THE TRUTH ABOUT THE MUSIC BUSINESS

WHAT EVERY ARTIST NEEDS TO KNOW BEFORE
THEY SIGN A RECORD DEAL

CHRIS GREENWOOD

DEDICATION

I dedicate this book to all the artists and musicians fighting for their dreams with the desire to get their music out there. If your dream doesn't require a team, you're not thinking big enough. Whether that's a record labels team or you are hiring your own. You got this!

CONTENTS

Dedication — 3

Introduction — 7

PART ONE: Understanding Record Labels — 9

    Why Do You Want a Record Deal? — 9

    Independent vs. Being Signed — 12

    Working with a label — 15

    Being independent — 16

    Why Signing a Record Deal Is Like a Marriage — 21

    What a Record Label Is Looking for in an Artist — 23

    Truth Bomb: The Label Sees You as an Investment Not as an Artist — 32

    Negotiating the Highest Advance and Best Deal Possible — 34

    How You Get Paid from a Record Label (it's not so great) — 38

PART TWO: Different Types Of Record Deals — 43

    Wrapping up — 56

PART THREE: Record Contracts: What You Need to Know Before You Sign — 59

    The Advance — 62

    Royalty Rate — 65

    The Term (This cost me A LOT of money) — 68

    How Many Songs or Albums You're Committed

to Delivering	70
Territories	72
Perpetuity	76
Artist Product Purchases	78
Rerecording Restrictions	79
Artistic Control	81

PART FOUR: How to Submit Your Demo, Make Contacts, and Show You're Ready to be Signed — 85

Getting Your Demo Ready	87
Seeking Feedback	92
Making Contacts: Music Conferences and Events	95
How to Email a Record Label — And Get a Response	102
The Fortunes Are in The Follow Up	114
What to do if you get a 'No'	115

PART FIVE: PERSISTENCE PAYS — 119

My story	121

Additional Books by Chris Greenwood — 129

Courses and Resources by Chris Greenwood — 130

INTRODUCTION

Hi there, my name is Chris Greenwood, A.K.A Manafest.

I run an educational company called Smart Music Business. I call it "Smart" music business because I've already made all the dumb decisions for you so you can avoid them – like signing bad record deals.

As the artist Manafest I've sold hundreds of thousands of albums and millions of singles, and the majority of those were sold without the help of a label. I've signed record deals in India, Germany, USA, Canada, UK and South Africa – to name a few. Some of the deals were amazing, like the one I had with EMI Japan (now known as Universal Music) and I'd sign that deal again in a heartbeat. Other record deals you couldn't pay me a million dollars to re-sign, they were such bad experiences. I'm sure I've lost thousands upon thousands of dollars in royalties but I no longer lose sleep over it. I now control all my music 100% and choose not to get dragged into my past because my future and my dreams are in front of me, not behind me. And that goes for you too: wherever you are in your career as you read these words, your dreams are in front of you, and I want to stand by your side as you walk the path towards them.

CHRIS GREENWOOD

As you'll learn in the pages of this book, not all record labels or deals are bad. But if you don't have the tools, knowledge or the 20 plus years' experience like I do you can get taken advantage of very easily. My hope is to save you from making any hasty or uninformed decisions that will affect your music career for years to come. I know artists who've had to pause their careers for years at a time because they were stuck in a deal. I also know artists who had their dreams manifested and toured the world selling millions because of a label as well.

So, get excited, strap in, and let's take a ride through this crazy music industry and get you prepared before a record contract lands in your hands.

PART ONE:
UNDERSTANDING RECORD LABELS

WHY DO YOU WANT A RECORD DEAL?

"You don't want the biggest record deal as far as money goes, you just want to make sure that the people at the label really support your band and the music and stuff."
— *Adam Rich*

I have a question for you before we really get started. Here it is:

Why do you want a record deal?

Think about it for a moment. Think about what you want a label to do for you that you can't do on your own.

Do you want a record deal because you want fame? Is it because you want to make a ton of money? Do you want to tour the world, get on TV, and have your songs on the radio?

Maybe you have your sights set on a specific label, either because they represent a bunch of artists you look up to, or because you feel aligned with their ethos and the impact they're making in the industry.

Or maybe it's just always been your dream to get your music out there, and you'd love the support of a team working behind you while you become famous and make a ton of money doing what you love.

Every one of these is a valid reason and if you feel that passionately about your dream I salute you. I am a big supporter of anyone with a dream — especially when they have the motivation to make that dream a reality.

Some of what you want from a deal you can do for yourself independently; some of it you might really need a label for. We're going to take a deeper dive into the pros of working with a label and the pros of going it alone in a moment, so don't worry if your ideas are vague right now.

The reason I'm asking you to dig a little deeper and look at why you want a record deal is because sometimes we get lost in the chasing of our dreams. We get so focused on going after what we want — especially when we've wanted it for a long time — that we don't really take a minute to think about why we want it.

Getting clear on what you want from a record deal puts you in a stronger position from the outset. When you couple that clarity of vision with the ground we're going to cover in this book, you're dynamite. You'll have so much more knowledge and awareness of what partnering with a record company can do for you (and what it can't) that when you're offered an opportunity you'll be able to make a decision and advance towards your dream from a truly informed place. You'll know what you want from a deal — so when one is put in front of you and what you want isn't included, you can ask for it, or walk away.

Usually, when I ask up-and-coming musicians why they want a record deal, there are two major reasons: the exposure, and a monetary advance. Advances are great if you don't have the finances to fund making your own record — but not every deal includes one, and they're not always of the five or six-figure variety. And while it's true that labels can bring exposure, if you want that on an international level you need to sign with a major label with offices in most or all territories.

If you've been researching the industry yourself what I just highlighted might be old news to you. And while we're going to go much deeper as we venture through the book, I just wanted to flag those two points up because back when I was starting out those were the kind of things I had no idea about. I didn't have a book like this to go through and my knowledge of the industry was pretty slim. When the time came for me to sign a deal, I was so caught up in the chasing of my dream that I was willing to sign whatever was put in front of me. Shocker: I signed a really crappy deal! But it got me started and I got out of it and I leaned a lot. Now I'm independent and I'm doing great.

You don't have to know the industry inside-out before you step into it, but having some clarity on what you want, and what you can expect, puts you at an advantage from the get-go. Next we're going to take a deeper dive into what a record deal can offer you, and what going independent can bring to your career.

INDEPENDENT VS. BEING SIGNED

> *"I was an artist, I was executive producer on my first album, so I've always had to manage both. I couldn't get a record deal. It wasn't by choice — I couldn't get a record deal, so I had to figure it out."* — Jay-Z

As you know, I've lived — and left — the label life, and now I'm fiercely and proudly independent. As such, I know the joys and frustrations of both worlds, and I'm happy I've forged a way of working and sharing my music that is right for me. Please know I'm not here to tell you which way you have to go: your journey is your own, and there are many paths to success. Even though I'm independent now, I still know and appreciate the value of what the right record contract can bring to an artist. It's my aim here to pass my knowledge of both camps on to you, so that you have balanced, realistic, and up-to-date information about each route.

Next we're going to take a closer look at these two worlds: the pros and cons of being signed with a label, and the risks and rewards of going it alone as an independent artist.

Before we do, I'm just going to lay out a few terms that will feature on the coming pages and throughout the rest of this book. If these concepts are new to you, please don't spend too long trying to get your head around them. By the time you've finished the whole book I'm sure that your understanding will have deepened — certainly enough to make your move into looking for a deal or treading the independent path.

Master recording and rights

The master recording is the original sound recording of a song; the master rights are the rights to the ownership of the sound recording of that song.

Master royalties and publishing royalties

When a physical sale, download or stream of a song or album takes place, two royalties are generated: master royalties and publishing royalties. Master royalties go to who controls or owns the master, and publishing royalties go to the songwriters of that particular song — and, if you have a publishing deal, whoever you have that deal with. While master royalties cover your music sales, publishing royalties are generated every time your song is played in public, for example on radio, plus any placements you get in TV, film or advertising (these are known as 'syncs' — see below for more).

Royalty checks are paid twice a year, but if, like me, you're a songwriter you also get quarterly checks for the publishing. If you distribute your music independently through places like DistroKid or TuneCore, then you get paid weekly for the master sales. But more on that later. Publishing royalties are typically paid in February, May, August and November, and always on the 15th.

Synchronizations (or syncs)

This is the term used for the process of having one of your songs or compositions used in connection with a moving picture. That covers film, TV, advertisements and video games — basically anything with a visual platform.

Great — now we've got those terms defined, let's start by getting an overview of the world of the signed artist vs. the world of the independent artist.

WORKING WITH A LABEL

When you sign with a label, you get their whole marketing machine working for you — and at a major label that machine is colossal, and it has a wide reach. Major labels have pre-existing relationships with radio stations, with advertisers, and with the film and TV industry. They can also support you with touring opportunities and distribution – both online and physical. While it's true that independent artists can still hook up with music supervisors (check out Sync Summit — it's an incredible resource) there are just some relationships that are easier, smoother and quicker to forge with a label behind you. Likewise if there are other artists on your label that you want to work with, the relationships and connections are already in place to get you collaborating.

When you sign with a label, you're immediately part of a whole structure and a system which wants to make you a success. It's amazing when you get that type of a deal and that level of attention — and it's even better when you're given an advance to make your record.

A label will also help you get on tours and get you in front of some big crowds. In short, working with a label can quantum-leap your career.

Do you sense a 'however' coming up?

The truth is, not all deals were created equal, and not all labels are as invested and supportive of their artists as they should be. Sometimes artists fall through the cracks, especially in big record companies. They don't get the attention that was promised upon the initial signing, and find themselves a little adrift.

Worse still is when an artist signs with a label and gets shelved. Depending on what's in the contract (and depending how good their lawyer is) an artist could find themselves in a position where their records just aren't being released, and they can't release any records on their own. Always be careful what you sign, and make sure there's a clause that lets you out of your deal if albums don't get released by a certain date. I have a ton of advice to share with you about the ins and outs of contracts coming up in Part Three.

A less serious, but still frustrating, fact about labels is that a lot of them are huge companies with many departments, so they take a while to make decisions. And when they do make decisions, you might not agree with them. If you don't like people telling you to make changes to your songs, your artwork, or telling you to work with certain people — signing with a label might not be for you.

BEING INDEPENDENT

In essence, when you're independent, you're not beholden to anyone. Your voice is your own: you can say whatever you want, and you can write and release the songs that really mean something to you.

You have full control of your release schedule: you can put out as many songs or albums as you wish, and you can release them frequently or far apart — it's your call. It's worth noting here that this can also work to your detriment, because some independent artists tend to release too many songs and miss out on the most important step – marketing and promotion. That's just something to keep in mind; don't overload your release schedule to the extent that you spread yourself way too thin and your songs don't get the attention they deserve.

Another pro about being independent is that you can collaborate with as many different artists as you like, and if you choose to tour — you can do it on your own terms.

Having that level of control of your career is very empowering. But we're missing the main pro of being independent: you own your own songs, 100%. You don't have to give 50% away to a label. You don't have to give part of the royalties away when your song is played on the radio. You control the masters, you own the publishing, and you have full rights when you sign and approve TV/Film placements.

Don't get being independent and going it alone mixed up: you can build a team around you by signing with a manager and by hiring publicists and radio promoters. You can also work with a booking agent and pay to go on tour with other, bigger acts in your genre — meaning you'll be in front of a ready-made audience who are most likely into what you do.

Do you sense the 'however' moment coming up for going independent? The obvious drawback is that without a label, you need to self-finance a lot of what I just laid out. Naturally, this can be discouraging for some artists. But here's my take: when you put the cash up front, you get paid up front.

Can you work a day and/or night job like crazy for a year while you save the money you need to record your own music and put it out there yourself? Depending on the producer you hire it might cost you $500-$5000 to record and produce your first track. Then you need to have a separate budget for marketing and promotion. Sometimes I negotiate with the producer to give him 50% of the master royalties if he'll produce it for free. This is a great way for you to get started independently without signing a deal or digging deep into your pockets. If this is all new territory for you please don't get overwhelmed at this point! Check out my book *How to Write and Release Your First Song* for an in-depth look at this process.

Know that there are always ways to cut costs. I'm blessed to have a talented wife who's also a graphic designer; she's responsible for the artwork on many of my best-selling albums and several of my books. But she has a career of her own too, so when she's busy I hire other folks to work with me. You really don't need to break the bank here: try websites like Fiverr, Upwork or 99 designs where you can hire talented designers. Alternatively, find someone in art college who would be happy to practice their skills and not expect professional rates just yet. If my wife and I are in a crunch to release a new single and need artwork fast, we'll hop online and search for some royalty free images on pexels.com or unsplashed.com. You can look like a pro without the massive budget. Just make sure to give credit to the photographer or designer. If you're looking for design and have a budget visit Visioncityart.com for package rates.

Another option for anyone looking to self-finance making their own record and meeting the marketing costs is to apply for a loan. If you choose to do this, use the loan to get your music out there — and when you've paid the loan back you'll still own your music — unlike when you pay back a record label advance from your royalties and you still don't own the music. They own it, and if you signed a traditional or 360 deal, they take a cut from 100% of the income streams it generates.

And while I don't encourage going into debt, see this approach as an investment in yourself. I'd rather you put up the risk and get the reward than the label. And who better to take a risk on than yourself?

Going independent isn't for everyone. So many artists don't make it because if the first record doesn't take off, they quit. This is where the experience of a label comes in: they know they won't break even until the second or third record, but by then they have an asset for life earning them income.

The fact is, if you go the independent route, you'll hit roadblocks. In particular you'll find it harder to get radio play, because, sadly, radio isn't about playing and sharing great songs — it's a political game. Put simply, labels rule the roost when it comes to who gets airtime, and independent artists will struggle against that force.

From my experience, even with the stations that were super supportive, a time comes when they succumb to what labels want them to play. One station in particular played one of my tracks regularly for a couple months (generating over $40,000 on Sound Exchange royalties alone) only to pull it because the labels were pressuring them to play their songs, instead of "This indie artist Manafest" — and that's an actual quote! Thank God radio isn't the only way to market an album anymore and we have dozens of other avenues, like social media, YouTube, TikTok, and TV and Film.

By now, I'm sure you're getting the picture that if you go independent you need a certain level of resilience, and you need to be ready to invest both money and time in yourself. It's a risk, no doubt about it. And I get it — but having made this route work for myself, I know that hitting it big on your own terms is one of the most liberating and satisfying things you can do. I also know that when the label system works, it works amazingly, and feeling supported and part of a team at a record company is incredible.

Ultimately, there's no one-size-fits-all way to work as a musician and share your music with the world. We live in an age of opportunity where the gate-keepers have less control, where there are more ways than ever before to get your music out there — and also where there's more competition to be heard than ever before. But I believe there's room for all of us, and the path you walk is yours.

WHY SIGNING A RECORD DEAL IS LIKE A MARRIAGE

"Find someone who has a life that you want and figure out how they got it. Read books, pick your role models wisely. Find out what they did and do it." — Lana del Rey

I love the analogy that signing a record deal is like signing the marriage register. I think it makes it crystal clear why it's important to put time and effort into any decision you make about teaming up with a record label and signing a deal.

Like marriage, it's a relationship where there is give and take. Both sides are equal, and both sides have needs and requirements that have to be met in order for the union to be a successful one.

The marriage analogy also gets across how serious signing a record contract is. Think about it — if you're looking to get into a long-term relationship with someone, would you date that person for a while, and get to know each other, or would you go on one date and then ask them, "Hey, do you want to get married? I know zero about you — but let's do it! Where's the nearest wedding chapel?!"

You wouldn't enter into that kind of commitment on a whim so why would you quickly sign with a label for three to seven years — or longer? You need to know you're compatible, and you need to know what the label's intentions are with one of the most precious things in your life: your music. And just like marriage, a record deal can be painful to get out of once you've made the commitment.

When you're offered a deal, take the time and court the person or the team you're communicating with. Get to know as many of the team as you can, from the A&R to the president and all the people in between. The reason you're coming together is so that you can accomplish something you can't on your own. Before you do that, you want to make sure they're the right fit for you. Find out which other artists are signed to the label and see what their experience has been, and what kind of a career they've had — especially those in your genre.

Why not release a couple of singles together to see how it goes? And if a certain amount of streams is reached (or another sales goal) then give them the first right of refusal to another single. That way, since they invested in you, if it takes off they get to blow your success up even further. However – if it tanks, then you can both walk away unscathed.

Don't lead purely from your heart by rushing to sign just because it feels like someone believes in you. I know what it's like to want someone to believe in you, but signing a deal is a time for wisdom and discernment. And, thanks to the time you're putting into research right now by reading this book, you'll be in a position where you can be discerning. By preparing now you'll be less pressured when an opportunity arises.

Your key question will always be:

Is the deal I'm being offered the right one for me?

Keep that in mind.

If not, don't sign. Trust your gut, trust your knowing. Wait for a deal that is right for you.

WHAT A RECORD LABEL IS LOOKING FOR IN AN ARTIST

"The roughest roads often lead to the top."
— *Christina Aguilera*

From the outside, record companies can seem like mysterious set ups. Knowing what they're looking for in an artist might seem elusive, or like a closely-guarded secret. In truth, it's actually pretty straightforward. Let's demystify this whole area and uncover the six things I've learned labels are looking for.

The number one thing a record label is looking for is hit songs

...And those songs need to be finished or 90% of the way there. The less work a label has to do to get a song finished and ready for release the better.

Your career begins with great songs: great songs that can be marketed to a big audience, that can be played on the radio, marketed online, and that you can perform. The label is looking for the hit song they can mass market to a global audience and generate revenue from via sales, streams and TV/Film synchs.

If you don't have songs that are ready and have the capacity to be a hit, then it's too early to reach out to a label. Same goes for a manager, if you're looking for one. The first thing they'll say is, "Let me hear the songs." Hit songs are the foundation to a successful music career.

I've been on both sides of the coin on this one. I've been the guy playing different songs for a label A&R and trying to explain the story behind each song, only to be stopped abruptly and told, "Just play me the hits." The A&R rep wasn't interested in my backstories or my inspiration at that point, he wanted to hear my best songs — the ones we could release to radio and promote.

And I've also been the guy hanging out with up-and-coming musicians who are sharing their music with me, playing song after song, giving me the backstories, and I'm thinking, "Just play me your best song!"

Right now, you might be thinking, *all my songs are good!* And I'm not here to rain on your parade, but the fact is the labels want to hear the standout track that's going to blow up your career.

When I look back on the last 20 years, I can see very clearly the individual songs — the hit songs — that accelerated my career.

Impossible blew me up in Japan selling 10,000 albums a week.

Avalanche blew up on US radio opening up massive tour opportunities.

Every Time You Run got me my first Top 40 hit in Canada.

It was always a new hit song that opened more doors than anything else. Albums don't sell albums, hit songs sell albums.

And, if we can fast-forward a little here, when you're promoting a hit song – make sure you have another lined up. Remember you're only as successful as your last song. So never stop writing and creating – even while you're riding the momentum of success.

The second thing a label is looking to see is if you're marketable

The label wants to sell you in order to sell your music. You're not just an artist, you're a brand, and they'll be looking to see how they can market you. They'll be interested in your look — are you good-looking, stylish, edgy? Beyond that they'll want to know if there's a cool angle or story about you they can work with. How did you get started? If you're a band, how did you come together?

Everyone loves a good story, and it gives you an edge when it comes to getting media coverage. Stories matter. Stories transcend everything.

Part of my story was I had a suicidal father and grew up in a single home. To handle my anger issues, I turned to rock music, hip hop and skateboarding. I got in a skateboarding accident in downtown Toronto while filming my best tricks on camera, and this accident took away my childhood dream of a pro skateboarder while also birthing a new dream of being a songwriter and performer. I tell that story over and over at live shows, in interviews, and I've definitely written about it in numerous songs.

If you haven't written your story down, write it now!

Touring is super important

If you're coming to a label to get signed, they're going to want to know your draw — in other words, how many tickets can you sell? Have you played any shows? Have you done any tours, if so how many, and who with? If you've got these things under your belt, that's going to set you apart big time. And that's what a label is looking for because touring drives sales and awareness. Not all artists have to tour, but if you can couple hit songs with promoting them via a tour then that puts you at an advantage.

One of the main ways artists get signed, especially bands, is when an A&R is invited out to see them play. This is the perfect way to court each other. The label can get a feel for the band, the fans, and start building that relationship. That was how I was originally signed – by setting up a showcase where the label came out to see the band and then we had talks afterwards. I blew away the president of a record label live and even hung out with him before the show. Unfortunately, I dragged him into a meeting with my so-called artist friends who almost ruined the relationship by asking rookie questions about music video budgets, making us all look ignorant about the business. I share more about that story in my book *Fighter: 5 Keys to Conquering Fear & Reaching Your Dreams.*

In essence, if you want to sign with a major label, touring is a big part of the music business and record selling business.

Labels are very interested in your social media numbers - and design matters, too

First, when it comes to social media, labels want to know what kind of engagement you have in order to see if you already have a fanbase. You might be noticing a trend: anything that you already have in place is less work for the label. Every hit song finished, every tour you've done, every show you've played, all your followers on Instagram, any photo shoots you've done, any logos you've had designed — they're all assets.

I just want to make a couple of points about the importance of not neglecting design and branding when you're looking to get signed. I talked a little about design for independent artists a few pages ago, but it's just as essential for anyone looking to get signed; labels don't hear you first – they see you first.

Pay attention to the look you're putting out there. If you're handing someone a demo, you really don't want it to be a blank CD with the name of your song written across in a Sharpie. These days it's more likely you'll be handing out MP3s, in which case a dope looking USB can go a long way.

I attended a music conference once to meet music supervisors and handed everyone I met a Skateboard USB flash drive loaded with my best songs written for TV/Film. I was sitting at a round table with one music supervisor and five other artists begging for their attention. The music supervisor took time to say, "Now that's how you get someone's attention and stand out." I walked away with his real contact info because I came prepared and stood out with a wow presentation.

You can also embed your single cover into an MP3, so when they hit play, the image pops up. If you're pointing people to your website – make sure the branding and design is consistent. If you're sending links to YouTube, make sure the music videos you're creating are aligned with the rest of your design and image. Show people that you care about design, and your art, and how your music is presented.

When it comes to social media, it's true that the numbers matter. Likes, followers and subscribers all help your case – but it's the relationship you have with those numbers that gives you an edge. Engagement is key here: some artists have a huge Instagram following but when they post there's little engagement. It's better to have 10,000 followers with hundreds of comments, than 20,000 followers and only a few likes or comments. Engagement shows you have fans, real fans, fans who care about what you're doing and want to connect with you. That's powerful.

My advice is to hone in on a couple of platforms and build audiences there. Choose the platforms you find the most fun, and go from there. It's better to be killing it on, say, YouTube and Facebook, than spreading yourself too thinly on every social media platform available and only having mediocre or low numbers and engagement to show for it.

The other thing I'm always preaching to my Fanbase University coaching students is to build an email list. I also encourage you to get a website with the dot com domain name. Even if it's just one page with links to your music, videos and tour dates, it shows you're serious. It shows you've invested into your career before asking anyone else to.

Labels want to gage if you're hardworking

When it comes down to it, the music industry is a lot of hard work. Getting up early, sometimes for interviews, scheduling flights, photoshoots, getting songs written, getting them recorded and submitted on time for deadlines — it's all work. As is going on tour, connecting with fans, responding to comments, signing autographs, all that stuff. Are you willing to put in the hard work?

Because if the record label is going to invest in you, they want to know that you're going to put in the work too. It's a 50-50 partnership.

In short, they want to know that you're motivated and willing to do whatever it takes to be successful.

And finally, labels want to know if you're easy to work with

Though it's last on this list it's actually the most important way to ensure success in any industry. No one wants to work with a jerk. No one wants to work with someone who's high maintenance, overly negative, and always complaining. There are certain people I've avoided working with because I had a bad experience with them, and there are people I've loved working with and have hired over and over. I'll never forget how comfortable a studio engineer named "X" made me feel when tracking vocals. Not only was he cool in tracking the record but when I had a few changes to make on the final product he was super cool about it. He didn't give any push back or attitude, even if he didn't agree with my change requests.

Labels want to work with people that are kind, cool, and easy to get along with. And you know what? If you're making a ton of money for them, yes, they'll put up with a mediocre or even bad attitude for a while. But let me tell you this: if you stop making money and you're still being a diva or a rock star jerk, you're done. They'll cut you off so quick. People don't have time for poor attitudes.

The best advice I can give you is to be kind to people. You meet the same people on the way up as you do on the way down. Kindness, showing up on time, paying people promptly — all of this will serve you well for a long time. As much as your website and engagement levels are an asset — so is your attitude, and so are the relationships you'll build. Relationships are everything in this business and your reputation is all you've got. They can take everything else away. But if you've got a good reputation and you have contacts, people will want to work with you.

And they'll want to help you out. They might not even love your songs right away. Maybe you might not have all those other pieces of the jigsaw that they're looking for, but if you're easy to get along with and they sense your passion and commitment, they'll want to help you develop your career.

Abraham Lincoln said, "I will prepare, and my opportunity will come." One day, your opportunity is going to come, but the question is will you be ready? Revisit the list we just went through and take stock of where you are. For anything that isn't in place, set some goals and start working towards them.

TRUTH BOMB: THE LABEL SEES YOU AS AN INVESTMENT NOT AS AN ARTIST

"The record business. It's exactly what it is: Record business. You have to take care of both, or they won't take care of you." – Dr. Dre

In the eyes of the record company, you're not an artist — you're an investment. That's the way record labels and the system defines you. They see you as a number, especially in the major label system. They're beholden to stockholders, and when it comes down to it, they're a corporation trying to see whether you make money. You're just another line on a spreadsheet and the question attached to your name is, "Do you make us money, yes or no?"

When I was signed to a label, I remember one meeting I had with the A&R where they told me they'd recently cut some artists from their roster. And do you know how they decided who to cut? The president of the label had a list of artists they were considering letting go, and he went through the names one by one. My name was on that list, and when he eventually came to me, he stopped and said, "Oh, Manafest, don't drop him, he makes us money. Next."

I make him money. That's why I didn't get dropped. I'm glad I made him money; that label opened up some huge doors for me and I'm grateful. But I wasn't saved from being dropped because they were so passionate about the music I was making, or because I'm such a nice guy. It was a purely financial decision.

This is the music business; the word business means profit. The key question for a label is always going to be, *Will this artist eventually be a positive return on the investment we're making?*

While it's true that most labels have some really nice guys who work in the A&R department who love music and who'll go to your shows — they're not the owners of the record label. They're good guys who have a passion to work with artists and be part of their development and journey in getting their music out there. But they're not the top guy, and they might not even have full signing authority.

If I was running a label, I'd want it to make money too, otherwise I wouldn't be able to keep it running.

So many artists get disillusioned when they're not generating a profit and quit before they even get to the point where they can show a label what an asset they could be. They think it's not working when really they need to invest more time and promotion in their careers. This is another reason why labels win: they have deep pockets and they know they might not break even or start making profits until an artist's second record. You have to have the stomach to invest – just like any other business owner – from the ground up. There is nothing wrong with honest capitalism. If you choose to be part of that system, it's better to swallow the pill now that first and foremost — you're an investment. Show that you're a good investment.

Record labels love working with artists who have already got some momentum behind them — that way they can pour on the rocket fuel and shoot you to the moon.

NEGOTIATING THE HIGHEST ADVANCE AND BEST DEAL POSSIBLE

> *"In life, you don't get what you deserve, you get what you negotiate."* — Dan Lok

Next we're going to look at how to negotiate the best deal possible when a record label offers you a contact. That means negotiating the best royalty rate, the best terms, and the highest advance.

You don't get the best deal by taking the first offer you're given — just like when you buy a house or a car. The first offer is a starting point. You hear it, and you put forward your counter-offer.

If you're a new artist, that might not come easy to you. You might be a little over-eager to sign, and if you are, that's usually for two reasons. The main one — and I really understand this — is that you're excited that someone believes in you enough to want to sign you. Been there, felt that! The other is that you might have hang-ups about the act of negotiating, maybe thinking it makes you appear obnoxious, or that it could be taken as rude. But there's a way to negotiate without being rude or obnoxious. And if someone gets offended because you pushed back on a few things, or asked questions for clarity, then it's time to take a beat and ask yourself if they're the kind of people you want to work with.

Having said all of that, I don't recommend you pick apart every minor point in the contract, you'll drive up everyone's lawyers' fees and test everyone's patience. Find the balance: be smart, be kind, be cool.

I remember when I was offered my first deal — I was so pumped. I took it to mean that someone believed in me; they liked my music enough to offer me a contract. I was totally heart-led. My objective and rational mind did not get a look in! I was so keen I almost signed straight away, but luckily I knew a few people in the industry, and so I asked them to look the contract over. Thank goodness I did, because unlike me, they saw it from an objective, rational head-led space — and it was a terrible deal. If I'd signed it, I would've been ripped off in a big way. It was all about what the label would get and what I wouldn't get. I thank God I had the option to ask for those experienced opinions on the contract — and I'm so glad that I can be that objective voice of experience for you now.

The truth is, there's almost always room for negotiation — you just have to know what gives you leverage. As we've looked at, there are ways of increasing your appeal — and therefore your leveraging power — when it comes to signing a deal.

To recap, when a label is weighing up whether they should sign you, they're looking at a lot of different things: first and foremost the songs you have ready, the 'hit' potential of those songs, and how quickly they can go to market. They're also interested in if you have live shows under your belt, professional photos ready, a logo, a website, a social media following, and an email list of fans already built up. All of these are assets that make you even more attractive, and put you in a position to negotiate a higher advance and better overall terms.

The next level of appeal would be if you've already started building a team around you, in particular if you have a manager and booking agent in place. By the way, if you have a manager, they're usually the ones who shop around for your deal; they act on your behalf as the middleman. While it's totally possible to negotiate without a manager, I strongly suggest you hire a entertainment lawyer who specializes in these types of contracts. Make sure anyone you hire specializes in entertainment law... Your Uncle's real estate lawyer is not the same thing!

I have to say, just by purchasing this book and educating yourself, you're going to be in a completely different head space than 99% of artists out there.

Now, let's address the most obvious stand-out aspect of any deal: the advance. The crux of it is that the size of the advance you're offered is a big indicator of how much a label believes in you. If you're offered a small amount like $5,000 to record the album and $5,000 for the marketing, I've got to be honest and say that's not a big investment for a label. As a rough guide, whatever you're offered as an advance, the label are thinking they'll be able to make ten times that amount back from your deal. The higher the advance, the more they believe in you and your potential for success. Labels are also looking for longevity, and the smart ones know that your first record might not break even — but it's the second or third that will. And, over the lifetime of the record, they'll continue to make money.

When I signed my first deal, I didn't get an advance. That's because I had nothing really to negotiate back then. I'd only toured in Canada, and had no real sales history other than 2,000 albums. I had no radio history except a few local stations that no one cared about. I was in a prime position to be taken advantage of — and I was — except that the deal I signed was a licensing deal, so at least I got to own my masters again ... after seven years. More on that later in the book.

Before I signed, I was making $70,000 a year in my day job. Looking back, with the gift of hindsight and the knowledge I've gained since then, I see I could've stayed independent for longer. I could have continued to invest my own money in my career to keep building my success, then started reaching out to the labels when I had more assets. I'd have been in a stronger position which would have allowed me to ask for an advance and negotiate much better terms overall.

When I think of the show *Shark Tank*, where you have investors that offer small businesses hundreds of thousands of dollars for only 5-10%

of the company, I see how crazy I was to sign that deal. I gave away 75% of my music for no investment at all. It's absolutely insane when you think about it, but yet it happens to artists in the music industry all the time.

This is why I recommend you view your career as something you are growing and cultivating. Believe in yourself enough to invest in it every day. Keep growing your fanbase. Keep taking action. As much as I'm a big believer in learning from those who've walked the path you want to walk by reading books, taking courses, seeking out mentoring — nothing beats raw experience. What if you put some songs out there by yourself? You could release and market a whole record and learn from all the mistakes. You don't learn how to swim by reading books about it, you learn by getting wet.

And if a record deal is what you ultimately want, see this like building up equity in a company. That way, when a label wants to partner with you, the value you represent is clear and undeniable.

HOW YOU GET PAID FROM A RECORD LABEL (IT'S NOT SO GREAT)

"Whatever excites you, go do it. Whatever drains you, stop doing it." — Derek Sivers (Founder of CDBaby)

THE TRUTH ABOUT THE MUSIC BUSINESS

I just want to take a moment to look at the financial reality of how you get paid from a record label versus how you get paid when you're independent. This was an area I didn't fully understand when I signed, and it lead me to some choices I wouldn't recommend — namely quitting my job too soon.

The most important thing you need to know is that labels pay you in quarterly installments. This was a huge shock for me; I went from having a regular salary from my day job, plus the weekly income from my record sales via the digital distributors I used, to getting paid four times a year. Being brutally honest, leaving my day job was like financial suicide on my part. I talk about that full experience in my book *Fighter: 5 Keys To Conquering Fear & Reaching Your Dreams*. I wasn't prepared for the financial hit I took — not at all. But you can be.

Independent artists can rely on regular income because they're paid weekly from their digital distributor (e.g. TuneCore, DistroKid, CD Baby) plus any other income streams they have going, such as the ad revenue from a YouTube channel. It's worth pointing out that when you're independent you get ad revenue for any YouTube videos that feature your music — not just the ones on your own channel. It's not unusual for around 70% of my YouTube revenue to come from the thousands of videos other people make that feature my music. Some of these videos even have more views then mine! For more info on YouTube royalties and growing your channel, pick up my book *YouTube Playbook for Artists & Musicians*.

The other aspect of a record deal that artists need to get wise about is the advance. I want you to really understand what an advance is and what it isn't. An advance is essentially a loan. Its purpose is to fund the making of your album, because you have studio costs to meet, and often marketing costs too. If you're in a band you might need to buy new instruments, drumheads, new guitar strings, plus whatever other sound gear you require to make your record.

If you leave your day job, like I did (only I didn't have an advance!) your advance also has to cover your living costs: rent, mortgage, bills, groceries... everything.

Then, when you're signed, once your record is made and finally comes out, any money it makes goes towards paying off that advance. This can come as a surprise to some artists — but the advance is exactly what it sounds like: it's an advance payment. It's not a bonus. You have to earn it and pay the record label back, and to pay it back you need to sell a ton of records, and until you do you'll only see money from touring and publishing. I remember it took a few years and a couple of records released before I felt like the checks every quarter actually amounted to anything.

In between royalty payments I was touring my butt off to keep the money coming in. Eventually I got some radio hits and that lead to an income increase, in particular when I started to get royalties from SoundExchange who deal with digital royalty streams. I won't go deep into this here — but when you start releasing music, make sure your songs are registered with a performance rights society and SoundExchange.com.

When it comes to the advance it's also important to note that unlike a mortgage or loan you take with your bank for a house, where once you pay it back you own the house free and clear, in most record contracts even when you've paid the label back – you still don't own your own music and, in most deals, only get a small percentage of royalties, 20-30% if you're lucky. I'll repeat my suggestion from Part One again here: why not get a loan from a bank, or ask a family member or friend to invest you? When you've paid it back you keep 100% of the business.

In essence, when you sign a deal, take the time to understand your contract — beyond the advance. Know how often you're getting paid.

Make sure you know how to budget and manage your cash flow. Don't just leave this up to a manager or anyone else on your team. Take control.

Don't rely solely on the quarterly payments. Build other income streams for yourself, whether that's from touring, or taking a day job, or starting your own online business.

The reason I recommend you don't just rely on royalties is because the hard truth is that unless you're selling hundreds of thousands of records, or getting millions of streams, your royalty checks aren't going to be huge. There are the anomalies: artists who have great radio success or get some big synch placements. It's definitely possible and I want you to aim big — but don't do what I did. Don't cut off your main income stream until you've built another to replace it first.

As we reach the end of Part One, I hope you're forming a picture of how the business side of the music industry works, and how you might choose to fit into that picture as an artist yourself. Whether you go with a label or go it alone, there will be deals to be done and contracts to sign — and that's where we're headed next.

PART TWO:
DIFFERENT TYPES OF RECORD DEALS

"The biggest risk a person can take is do nothing."
— *Robert T. Kiyosaki*

It's time now to take a deep-dive into the world of record labels and the different types of deals that are out there – both for signed artists and independent ones. We're going to focus on the five main ways you can work with a record label or distributor. Specifically, we'll cover:

- Traditional deals (sometimes called a standard deal, or a full album deal)
- Publishing deals
- 360 deals
- Licensing deals
- Distribution deals

My aim here is to give you an understanding of the many avenues that are available to you as a musician who wants to share their music with the world. I want to shine a light in the usually dark corners of the industry, so you are tooled up and in the know about what these deals expect from you, and what you can expect from them.

Let's start with **traditional record deals.** When you sign a traditional deal, the label owns your master recordings, and they usually have publishing rights to your songs too. They've invested money in you and the production of your songs; owning the rights to your music is how they recoup that investment back. How much they own, and how much you own, will depend on the specifics of your contract – we're going to look at contracts in more detail in Part Three – but for now it's enough to know they have the right to collect royalties for all the channels that currently exist, e.g. CD sales, vinyl sales, online streams — and also in those channels which are yet to be created.

When you sign a traditional deal, you'll get an advance, as we've looked at already. Another advantage is that you get plugged into the label's marketing machine. The label will organize songwriting sessions, help schedule photo shoots, hire a graphic designer, choose a producer, and set up either a radio tour to visit stations or book back-to-back interviews that coordinate with the release of your record. They'll get you more exposure via playlists and press, both online and in print.

The connections and power labels have when it comes to radio play cannot be underestimated.

They might also ask you to work on a particular track to make it more suitable for radio, or suggest another artist (hopefully one with a great profile) to feature on it. Personally, I'd listen to and appreciate this kind of input; I've seen the opportunities that follow after a radio hit. The momentum it brings to record sales — and ticket sales if you're touring — can really accelerate your career. Of course, if the label owns the master rights, you'll be sharing any money you make with the label. But, if they're the ones who get you the airplay, it's not such a bitter pill to swallow.

In a traditional deal, it's the label's job to make your record the best it can possibly be from the songs to the packaging, and while it's true that they'll work with you and include you in on most decisions — ultimately they hold the strings. In this way, they really are in control of every aspect of your career.

> *"What the big print giveth, the small print taketh away." — George Ross*

Publishing deals look after your songwriter rights. Most labels tend to deal with publishing rights as well as master rights, and in a traditional deal, the two areas will be covered in your contract. The only instance where an artist might seek a publishing deal only (and no other type of deal) would be if they're not looking to release songs under their artist's name, but instead just write songs for other people.

In short, when you sign a publishing deal, you grant a publishing company part ownership of the "songwriting" of your songs in exchange for the royalties they'll generate by exploiting your songs. They can do that via streams and sales, getting them played on the radio, or getting them placed in TV or film.

Now let's turn our attention to **360 deals**. Of all the kinds of deals out there, 360 contracts are the most exclusive. They grant the label a percentage of the earnings from ALL of an artist's activities, not just album or single sales. This includes income generated from touring, from merchandise sales, from your music being featured in a game or in a commercial, even from TV appearances — plus they'd have publishing rights, masters rights, and rights to royalties from any streams of income from your music which has yet to be invented.

If you're a brand-new artist and don't have anything going on in terms of income coming in or a fanbase developed, then the label needs to invest heavily in you to make you a success. Obviously, they're going to try to get a piece of everything in the deal so they get a return on their investment.

Here's the thing: if a record label is going to be participating in the benefits of a 360 deal, then they should be active in increasing your revenue in all those different streams. That means they should be bringing new and bigger opportunities to the table, and leveraging relationships and deals with people who you don't have access to without them.

They should be getting you crazy distribution by selling more albums than you can; getting off-the-charts online streaming numbers via big playlist placements; getting your music featured on TV and in films; getting you placed on awesome tours; getting you a merchandise deal where your t-shirts are sold across the nation in different stores, and generally — just blowing you up!

But, if they're not, and they're just poaching your income — walk away.

It makes me think of the Starmaker fund in Canada that gives grants to artists who have already achieved a certain level of success to market their music further. That is what the label should be doing: making you a star!

A 360 deal is either a guaranteed way for a label to invest in you and recoup that investment — or it's a big money grab for them if they don't bring any or all of those opportunities I listed above. I'd rather have 50% of a watermelon then 100% of grape. However, some artists sign to a label and end up splitting 50% of a grape because the label didn't do anything to build or further their career.

Personally, I would never do a 360 deal unless the label was going to increase my revenue ten fold. For example, if you can make an annual revenue of $100,000 from your music independently, and a 360 deal could make you $1,000,000 — then it'd be something to consider. But even in that case, I would want a clause written into the contract which states if the label doesn't create X amount of revenue by a certain date, they no longer have rights to my music.

If you find a 360 deal in front of you, understand what you're giving up when you sign. You might write a book in five years time — and you'll have to give up some of the royalties on it depending on the contract. You might go into movies or acting — think Justin Timberlake, Eminem, 50 Cent — and you'll have to share your fee with the record company.

A 360 deal means they'll take a piece of every possible income stream you make as an artist — and if it hasn't been invented yet they'll still want a piece of it when the time comes. NFTs (non-fungible tokens) have only just been invented and have become a massive source of income for artists, generating millions of dollars in a short period of time. If you don't have the rights to your music then you can't tap into these income streams.

The upshot of a 360 deal is that the label controls everything.

Let's turn our attention now to looking at what **a licensing deal** entails, which is what I signed back when I first started out, and later in my career too. With a licensing deal, you're granting the label the rights to produce, distribute, market and sell your music for a set period of time in territories where they have rights. It's worth noting that I didn't give up any of my publishing rights when I signed a licensing deal; in my case, the label didn't ask for them so I was unscathed. Because I'm a songwriter as well as a performer, that deal suited me well.

A licensing deal works great for artists who have an album or several albums professionally recorded and ready to release. It's also a good option for artists who have already started to make an impact on their scene but would benefit from being able to tap into the artist services of the label's in-house publicity team, who usually have relationships and links with radio stations.

As with a traditional deal, the label controls the master recordings — but only for the amount of time specified in your contract. Once the term is over, the rights return to you.

When I signed my first licensing deal, I signed my music over to the label for seven years —which was way too long! But I didn't know that back then. When it came to signing my second licensing deal I was much more prudent, that time signing over my records for five years. If you find yourself in a similar position I whole-heartedly recommend you consider signing for a shorter period such as three years, because it's usually in the first two or three years that the label will actively promote and push your music. After that their input slows down ... so why should they still make money from you?

Licensing deals tend to include an advance, but not always. I didn't get one for my first deal, but when it came to my second I was in a much better position to negotiate because I'd achieved a certain level of success by then. Not getting an advance the first time had one up-side – it meant that I got paid royalties faster because there was nothing for the label to recoup.

While it's true that licensing advances aren't usually as big as traditional deal advances, it's understandable because the label is doing a lot of work on your behalf. There's more risk involved for them. They're taking care of the manufacturing, distribution, and sales of your music. And hopefully they'll be doing what they can to market your music, secure radio airplay and generating all the publicity they can to help sell your record.

Here's an example of how that worked for me: years ago, the label I was with sponsored several different music festivals, which gave me the opportunity to headline some of those shows. They also partnered with a few radio tours, and again that connection put me in front of crowds I wouldn't have accessed on my own. The biggest upside was that I got distribution through EMI (now Universal Music), which cracked open the door to Japan. Even though the label was pushing their fully-signed artists, Japan handpicked me because my music and image worked for that market. This was like a dream come true proving that just having great music can still win over the politics of the industry.

The other upside of this was because my deal was a licensing deal, and not a 360 deal — the label didn't take a percentage of the income I made from doing these shows, or any of the money I made from merchandise. They just wanted me to tour and perform — in order to help sell my records. It was win-win.

Having said all of that — and I can only speak from my own experience of licensing deals — overall, I definitely noticed a difference in the level of support I got from the label versus how much support other artists with a traditional deal got. While this was frustrating at the time, I do understand it from the label's perspective: they only had rights to sell my records for a certain number of years (rather than forever like in a traditional deal) and because I didn't get an advance they didn't have a lot of skin in the game.

The takeaway from that experience is: the more a label invests in an artist, the more they'll treat them as a priority.

> *"The difference between mortgaging your music with a record label and mortgaging your house with a bank is at least you own the house once you've paid back the bank."*
> *— Chris Greenwood*

Finally, let's take a look at what a **distribution deal** is. If you're going the independent route, this is your deal. When you sign a distribution deal, you're responsible for creating your album, manufacturing any physical copies (CDs, vinyls, USBs) of your music, producing the digital master, and marketing it. You are also in charge of the shipping costs to the distributor. You'll want to consider hiring a publicist, a radio team, and have a good budget for online marketing to create awareness about your music and to encourage people to buy your record. So there's a lot of upfront cost involved — but this route gets you the most income back if your album blows up. You are in control of all of the income streams your record generates — because you control the masters.

The distribution company you sign with is responsible for uploading your music to all the digital online stores, and if it's part of your deal, they'll take care of getting your music delivered to physical retail stores. As you can imagine, the advancements in technology and the way we listen to music have undergone seismic shifts in the last ten years, and as a result physical distribution is less common.

Back in the day, the goal with retail stores was to get great placement on the shelves, ideally at the end of an aisle (an end cap) — and even better if there was a listening station so customers got a chance to sample your sounds.

Here's me in Tokyo, Japan, at a Tower Records. Note the great shelving space, complete with end cap and listening station.

THE TRUTH ABOUT THE MUSIC BUSINESS

These days, unless you have massive exposure, are touring, or have a radio hit in specific markets, there's little point in having physical distribution; it's a dying model.

On the other hand, digital distribution is very much alive and kicking. Companies like DistroKid, TuneCore and CD Baby allow artists to distribute their music to online retailers such as Apple Music, Spotify, Deezer and dozens more. Instead of striving for the Holy Grail of shelf space, the goal is now to get good digital placements. That can include getting onto a Spotify editorial playlists, or being featured in their 'Marquee' tool — essentially pop-up banners promoting your music to potential fans. Any indie artist who distributes digitally with DistroKid, TuneCore or CDBaby can pitch for this type of exposure with Spotify.

If you go with a distribution deal, I suggest discussing the prospect of pitching your songs for placement in Apple Music. You can get featured in your genre with a banner placement, like the one below. For this specific release, my album was featured in a banner in the top of iTunes/Apple Music under the Christian and Gospel genre.

If you'd like to know more about this, I go into more depth in my course *How I Make Over $10,000 a Month Selling Music Online.*

Something else I advise with a distribution deal — especially if you're going for physical distribution — is to do a deal in your own territory, because that's where you have the most control and the most contacts. If you're selling online, you can market to and from anywhere using Facebook ads or YouTube ads, or by hiring the people I've mentioned previously (publicists, radio promoters) who can help push your music.

When it comes to brokering international deals in different countries, be discerning. Don't just sign the first thing offer that comes your way. Check references, check with other artists. For example, if you want to get distribution in Germany, and you know other artists who are forging that path, ask who they recommend you work with. Then reach out to them via email (we'll be looking at how to reach out to labels and other industry professionals more fully in Part Four).

When my licensing deal ended with EMI Japan, I contacted a fellow artist in Japan I had worked with to ask if he knew of any indie labels that would distribute my record. Within a week I had a new distribution deal with a new label partner.

Of all the deals we've looked at, a distribution deal is the one that gives you the most autonomy. It's also the one that asks you to take the biggest risk — in order to reap the biggest reward. Remember everything is negotiable; I recently did a physical-only distribution deal in Canada and the USA, excluding online. I don't need this company for online, that's what DistroKid or TuneCore is for.

If you choose to strike out alone and seek out a distribution deal, and you have a sense of trepidation about it — welcome that feeling. This is you charting your own course. Anything is scary the first time you do it — but you learn by taking action.

WRAPPING UP

I hope that this journey around the main types of record deals has opened some mental doors for you, and shone a light on the possibilities that are out there. I hope you've seen beyond the idea that a 'big deal' is the only way to experience success in our industry. You might be getting the sense that a licensing deal would work well for you, or you might want to seek out a distribution deal. Or you might really want to get a traditional deal or a 360 deal — and that's totally cool, if that's what works best for you as an artist.

I believe there is wisdom in starting small, building your career, and signing with a label, for whatever type of deal, when you're ready. That way you can negotiate a great deal, reap the benefits, have an awesome working experience, and get out when the time comes. A record deal isn't the end of the journey — it's part of the journey.

You might choose to release an album on your own the first time, financing, marketing and launching it yourself so you can get the full experience. I actually think this is a really awesome place to start and a great way to learn about what works and what doesn't. Because once you've done it and you understand it — and especially when you make a success of it — you'll be in a much better place if a major deal comes knocking on your door. You'll understand so much about the process, and what to expect from a label's marketing machine. You'll be extra-motivated to make sure they're working for you, and representing you in the very best way.

And, please — before you sign any deal, I have to advise you again to get a good entertainment lawyer who specializes in the music business to look at any contract you're considering. Never be afraid to negotiate or ask questions — just do it professionally.

With that in mind, we've circled back around to one of the key pieces of advice I offered in Part One: whether you're part of a label's stable, or galloping out on your own like a wild horse — be cool to work with. Make sure your people feel valued and involved. The more you involve people in what you're creating, the more they feel invested and want to work harder for you. There were times when I had my licensing deal where I just delivered the songs to the label without asking for any input from my team, and I now see that was a mistake. People love to promote and champion things they felt they had a part in creating, whatever their level of contribution was.

Plus it makes the whole experience more meaningful and fun for you. And isn't that one of the reasons you want to be a musician? It's so much better when you're having fun, sharing your passion, and feeling the sense of elevation you get from working with awesome people who actually want the best for you. Whichever path you take, you got this.

PART THREE:
RECORD CONTRACTS: WHAT YOU NEED TO KNOW BEFORE YOU SIGN

Picture the scene: you've wanted a record deal for as long as you can remember. It's been your ultimate dream to work with a record company who are willing to team up and finance your journey so you can share your music with the world. And now, at last, you have a contract in front of you. Your eyes dart to the most important thing to you in that moment: the advance. Maybe you'll look at how many of your records they're going to put out. Maybe you'll look at the percentage of royalties they'll take.

But overall, how discerning will you be?

How much notice will you take of the small print?

And how likely are you to just think it'll all be okay, and everything will work out?

Is there a part of you right now thinking, *Why are you being such a downer about it all, Chris? This is my dream moment, get out of the frame!*

As you're this far into the book I'm confident you're already a lot more aware of the realities of a record deal, and you're more prepared to look a little deeper into any deal that comes your way. And that's really my goal here: to get you as aware and prepared as possible so you are in control of your own career path — especially when you're working with a label.

This next part of the book is where we go even deeper and look at some of the terminology you can expect to see in a record contract.

The truth is legal contracts can be overwhelming; they use specialized language and unusual phrasing that can make your head spin. It can be difficult to decipher and navigate these almost-alien documents on your own. Which is why my first piece of advice, and I will probably repeat it, and okay – I've already said it ... is to hire a lawyer to look at any contract you're giving serious consideration to. Not a real estate lawyer, not someone who does criminal law or corporate law — an entertainment lawyer. An expert in their field. You'll be paying for this service, so it makes sense to get the right service for what you require.

But it's not enough to just pass it over to someone else. I strongly advise that you educate yourself so you know what's being given to you, asked of you, *and taken from you* in a contract. That's what we'll focus in on next.

When you couple your own understanding with the specialized understanding of an entertainment lawyer, you will be in such an awesome position to negotiate a deal that works for you and will advance your career. I've mentored too many bands and artists who've neglected to read the small print in their contracts only to find themselves locked into a bad deal. I really do not want that for you!

By the way, if you're reading this as someone who's already signed a deal that you've come to realize isn't a great one — I suggest you also tool yourself up by reading the coming pages carefully, and that you too have an entertainment lawyer look over your contract to see if there are any workarounds. Your main focus should always be on furthering your career, so if you're stagnating in a bad deal get support as soon as possible and work out how you can continue making and recording your music.

Before we dive in, I just want to reiterate that I'm not here to throw shade on all record companies and all deals. Labels are an important part of the music industry ecosystem, and when you sync up and get the right deal for you, amazing doors open and opportunities are generated.

But the label is not more important than you. They're not more important than your art and your development as a musician. They're not more important than your fans and the people you can connect with via your music.

It's about co-creating, working together, and — crucially — not being taken advantage of. Contracts are prime areas for this to happen. I signed my first contract before it was commonplace to research and access information via the internet, so if there's anything on the coming pages that still seems a little blurry or abstract, you have the power at your fingertips to go deeper, to find out more, and to really put yourself in the driving seat.

No more excuses.

> *"A contract is between two people that mutually distrust each other. A covenant is between two people that mutually trust each other." — Myron Golden*

THE ADVANCE

For a lot of artists, the advance is the most glamorous and attractive part of a record deal — and I totally get why. It's definitely an important part of it; as we looked at in Part Two, the advance can be a reflection of how much the label believes in you and how much they're willing to invest in you. The question I would really like you to keep front and center when you're considering a deal that includes an advance is this:

What am I trading for this amount of money?

I want you to keep that in mind even if you're looking at an advance of six or seven figures. Even when that amount of money is on the table, you still need to take a pause and look at what you're being asked to give up. To really understand what you're trading, you need to know what the rest of the contract is asking of you, and that's why I urge you to familiarize yourself with the terms and language of record contracts.

First off, I'll share a few things it's useful to know about an advance, then we'll move on to what the uninitiated might think are the less glamorous aspects of a contract with a music label — but believe me — it's the uninitiated who get burned.

When it comes to receiving the advance, you usually get half of the money up-front, and the other half when you deliver the first record. Having said that, I recommend you look out for other clauses in relation to the payment of the advance: for example, do you need to sell a certain number of units before you get the rest of the money? And what's actually included in the advance? Are you expected to use some of the money for marketing, or is there a separate budget for that? Do they want to take a cut of your publishing rights as well?

Always remember the advance is a loan — the record company wants to recoup that money from you, and they do that by selling your record.

Let's say your advance is for $50,000. If your record sells for $10, you might think you need to sell 5000 units to pay the advance back —

but there are a bunch of expenses that get taken off that $10. For example, when it comes to digital sales, iTunes will take a 30% cut — so a $10 album makes the record company something closer to $7. Only it doesn't... because they'll have distribution costs to meet too. When it comes to CD sales, there are obviously costs involved in the manufacturing of CDs and the printing of inserts and so on.

We'll actually go into a little more detail on how much the record company (and you!) make from sales in the section that's coming up on royalties, but for now the main takeaway is that all of these expenses slow down the process of paying back the advance — which means it can take a while before you start to receive any money from royalties.

In essence, when your eyes dart to the advance, pay attention to when you get paid, how often you get paid and what the advance includes. Don't be afraid to ask for more especially if there's a bidding war going on and other labels are interested. However, if it's an indie label you don't want to take such a big advance that there isn't a budget left to promote and market the music – because then everyone loses.

Side note: Even though I was signed to a label with no advance, that never stopped me from putting my own money in constantly to market my music. I was looking at myself as a long-term investment. With or without the labels help, I was determined to make it.

When an advance is offered, always keep that question in mind: What am I trading for this amount of money? Keep reading to get more clarity on that.

ROYALTY RATE

As we covered in Part One, royalties are paid whenever your music is bought or streamed. They're paid to you, and they're paid to the record company, so when you're studying a potential contract you want to be looking out for what percentage you're getting, and what percentage they're taking. And, of course — you want to make sure you get a fair rate.

It's worth noting here that often when negotiating with a label, there are steps leading up to the contract being sent and you deciding if you sign or not; normally, the main points are negotiated over email first. In those cases, the biggest piece of advice I can offer you is get them to state their terms first. And when it comes to royalties, if they ask you what rate you're looking for, you can throw it back to them with questions like:

What's the standard deal that you tend to do?

What do you do in cases like this with most artists?

What kind of rate do you guys typically offer?

By getting them to show their hand first, you get to know where they're coming from. The last thing you want to do is go in low by asking for 40% when they were willing to give you 60%.

There are a few things to consider when it comes to how royalties are calculated. I touched on this a couple of pages ago, but I'm going to build on it a little more in terms of how royalties are worked out.

First of all, as we know, if your record sells on iTunes for $10, Apple will take their 30% cut right away. Of the remaining $7, a percentage will go towards distribution — and that can be anything from 15% to 25% — let's go with 20% for the purposes of our calculation. That's another $2 off your $10 record, leaving $5 in the pot. There might be other expenses to detract as well: label expenses, marketing costs, your manager's cut. Whatever is left — we'll say $3 — is then divided between you and the record company. If your royalty rate is 50%, you're looking at $1.50 per record. And if we take this same calculation and apply it to selling individual songs rather than albums, you get 15 cents every time someone buys your song.

By way of comparison, if you decide to go the independent route you only need to factor in two expenses from that $10: 30% to iTunes, and whatever you pay your distributor. Some independent distributors take a percentage per sale, like CDBaby (around 9% for digital sales) while others like TuneCore charge an annual fee. But the difference is … you get 100% of whatever's left. That's more like $6 per sale, instead of $1.50 per sale. Of course, you're going to funnel some of that $6 back into your business; when you're independent you have to meet marketing costs and so on that we've looked at already, but you have so much more control over where you channel your money.

This is one of the things that really struck me back when I'd get royalty statements from my old label: the lack of transparency in the numbers. I could see clearly how much I'd made — but the numbers were never broken down as to where they were coming from. I never saw a break down of the income streams from platforms like YouTube, Spotify, Apple, SoundExchange or TV/Film placements. I just had to trust that it was all above board. It's crazy when I think about it now, but back then I accepted it. It was part of the game. I just didn't know the rules back then.

In short, my key piece of advice on royalties echoes what I said in relation to advances: when a label is asking for a certain percentage of your royalties, what are they going to do for you to earn that royalty rate? Why should they keep 50, 70 or even 90% of the profits?

Again, we're not making labels the enemy here, but we're getting clear on the realities of what they're taking from you so you can negotiate from a more knowledgeable position. If you truly believe there is going to be a bigger pie with the label involved, then you should have no problem signing and allowing them to share in the success they helped create.

> *"It takes a team to do anything of lasting value." — John C. Maxwell*

THE TERM
(THIS COST ME A LOT OF MONEY)

As you might have got by now, I love helping artists avoid the mistakes that I've made. And, as I mentioned previously, one of the biggest mistakes I made was not paying full attention to how long the record company would own my masters for in the first licensing deal I signed.

I've talked about that first deal throughout the book but let me give you the basics for clarity now: it was a **three-album** licensing deal with a US label, with no **advance**, the **term** was seven years, and the label had the rights to sell my records in all **territories** apart from Canada. I don't recall the **royalty rate** — but it was low enough that it took a long time before I started to make any real money.

We're going to look at each of those areas of a contract (and more) in the coming pages, but right now we're focusing on that phrase: the term. This is the one element of both my first and second contract that I really wish I had paid more attention to. Essentially, the term is how long you're tied into the deal you're signing, or the length of time they have rights to sell your record for.

I thought I was signing a five-year term, which, to be honest, felt too long even when I was just a couple of years into the deal. But the time finally came when those five years were up, and I was stoked because I thought — at *last* — I was getting one of my best-selling records back. I emailed the label and asked them to take my albums down from all outlets, because I was ready to re-upload them and distribute them as an independent artist.

Then... the label emailed back to say they still had the rights.

I emailed them back to say no, the five years were up, so the rights would return to me.

And ... they replied with a copy of the contract I'd signed, highlighting the term was in fact seven years.

My stomach dropped. I felt sick. The records were still selling well, and I'd expected to have a much bigger stream of income coming my way because the rights were about to be returned — only they weren't. I was locked in for another two years. I've estimated those two years cost me tens of thousands of dollars.

You live and learn. And I learned that seven years is a long time. I recommend you aim for a three or four year term, max. As I've said previously, labels tend to cool down on promoting an album after a couple of years — so that's when you should get your records back. Simple.

HOW MANY SONGS OR ALBUMS YOU'RE COMMITTED TO DELIVERING

Another important part of a record contract you want to take note of is how many records, or how many songs, you're committed to delivering.

My first piece of advice here is that you look beyond the number and also check the time period (not the term, that's different) that ties in with this number.

For example, you could be obligated to releasing 50 songs at a rate of one every two months. Or, at the other end of the scale, you might only be permitted to release an album every two years. Those kind of restrictions can be easy to miss when you first look at your contract, so they're worth looking out for. You need to consider what kind of output you're happy with and capable of, and ensure the expectations in the contract are in alignment with that.

If you're offered a five-album deal, you might be tempted to put on the rose-tinted spectacles and think this means the label really believes in you... or you might choose to be cautious and realize that if you become super-successful, you're locked into this deal for the foreseeable future. If you're offered that kind of deal, it's worth considering how long it takes to write, record and release five albums; you're looking at a partnership that could last up to ten years, or even longer. Do you want to be tied in for that long?

Some deals are just for one album — and that's actually not a bad thing. It means if you don't like how the label work with you on that one album, you're not committed to making more with them.

Other deals can include what's termed as an 'option'. For example, if you sign a three-album deal, the label are only obligated to release the first, then if they're happy with it, they have the option to request a second, and then a third. It's essential to note that if you sign this kind of contract, you have to deliver those requested albums — no matter what your experience has been with the label so far. Seem a little one-sided? That's because it is!

If you don't feel comfortable with that, consider asking your lawyer to add a clause that stipulates that if, after one album release, certain goals or sales aren't achieved, you won't be making another album with the label. I've done this myself in the past and it's a wise way to protect yourself.

If asking for that clause scares you in any way, think of it like this: if a label is telling you they love your music and that they want to invest in you (and that's the message you should be getting from them) then it shouldn't be weird in any way for you to want to see evidence that they'll stick to their word before you commit to making more music for them.

Why wouldn't you want to work with a label again if they're doing an awesome job? You're on the same team after all.

And I just want to say that potential for team spirit does exist. It's not all horror stories out there! There are really great labels who have positive and harmonious working relationships with their artists, where everyone's working together with the same common goal: making you a successful artist. That should *always* be the goal.

TERRITORIES

The territories are the areas you agree the label can sell your music in. And straight up I'm going to say that if they want the rights to the whole world — then they need to be working hard to push your music all over the world.

As you might expect, a label based in the US is going to be pretty good at selling in the US. It's their home turf and they'll have a lot of connections and relationships set up there. But what about the rest of the world? Do they have connections in Japan, Germany, the UK? And if they don't, why do they want the rights to sell there? Well — to take more of your royalties, of course!

Before you give a label the rights to sell in any country except the one where they're based, you want to be getting clear on what their connections are in those countries. And if those connections are lacking, take those territories off the table. YOU can still sell your record and reach fans in those territories, by distributing your music yourself through DistroKid or TuneCore.

When I signed my first licensing deal with the US label, I gave them the rights to all territories except for Canada. I took Canada off the table so I could apply for some of the grants that are set up here to support artists, and I needed to be independent in Canada to qualify for those. I'm grateful that my lawyer helped me navigate that.

The reality of granting the label the rights to sell my music in every other country is that they didn't do anything for me in so many of those countries: the United Kingdom, France, Germany, and several others. It was actually during that deal that I blew up in Japan — but that was only because they had distribution through EMI, and EMI Japan happened to hear the record and love it. They promoted it and that was the reason why I became so successful over there; it was nothing to do with the deal I did with the label in the US. They still benefited from it — because I'd granted them the rights to sell in Japan. I share more about that whole story in Part Five of the book.

Recently one of my songs, *Edge of My Life*, started selling like crazy in China. This came as a bit of a surprise as it's almost seven years old. I started to notice all these AMV Japan type animation videos being made with the song and it transpired it was because of a sudden spike in the song's popularity in China and Taiwan. I was trying to understand why these Chinese record companies were emailing me offering to license the song. I finally responded to one of them and we almost had a deal in place until I did my due diligence of checking my royalty statements with TuneCore. I realized I was already making a ton of royalties from this song in China and getting paid because TuneCore had distributed my music there. I almost signed away the rights to a music company for a pittance for six years while what I was already earning monthly from this song in China alone was worth more.

The moral of the story is you can have a song blow up in a country you've never even toured in without the help of a record label. Just remember there's always a reason why labels are knocking on the door .. and it's not to be your friend. There was blood in the water so the sharks came hunting.

I ended up hiring a virtual assistant and translator who spoke Chinese to help me promote the song further in China without having to give up my rights to the song. We edited my lyric video and put Chinese subtitles to it and uploaded it to TikTok and other music platforms in China.

Something else to consider when you sign for the whole world: you have to buy your own CDs off of the label. I'm going to go over this in a more detail when I talk about the part of a contract that covers Artist Product Purchases, but for now I just want to make the point that if you sign for all territories and then you want to tour and sell your CDs afterwards, you have to buy them first from the label for around five dollars each. Yeah – you read that right!

Obviously, when you price your CDs for a gig you tend to go low because you're competing with the bar, and any potential customer is weighing up whether they should shell out five or seven bucks for your CD or just go and get a beer. Having to buy your CDs from the label leaves you with little or zero profit margin on your own album when you're touring. Which is kind of nuts! Luckily, because I maintained the right to sell my records in Canada I could press my own CDs for a dollar each — much more reasonable.

As a side note, one way to increase profits at a show and increase your average order is to give away the CD for free when someone buys a T-shirt. That way fans are a walking billboard for your brand and they're walking away with your music.

The only time a worldwide deal is worth it is when it's with a big label who are going to push you on a worldwide scale. I've seen this work really well, for example with the band Magic! whose lead singer helped me write some songs in the past. They signed with Sony Music Entertainment and the rights to all territories so the label worked hard to push their music in those territories. It was awesome to witness their rise to fame. And if you haven't seen the documentary *Artifact* with 30 Seconds to Mars, I encourage you to watch it. Jared Leto, the lead singer, talks about how behind any globally successful artist you'll find a globally successful label, because they're the labels who have the power and the connections to push that artist in every single country. I'm talking about major label deals here, where millions of dollars are channeled into catapulting artists like Drake, Katy Perry, Billie Eilish and Lady Gaga into the limelight.

The main lesson for us here and now is that if you're being asked to sign away all territories, you want to make sure you're asking the right questions about what the label is going to do in order to deserve those territories. Know your worth, and stand your ground.

PERPETUITY
(THE ONE WORD THE LABEL DOESN'T WANT YOU TO KNOW)

Remember in the intro to Part Three I noted how record contracts are full of specialized language and unusual phrasing? This word 'perpetuity' is a prime example of that. If a label is asking for the rights to sell or distribute your records in *perpetuity* — it means forever.

Just take that in. It's your work, your art, your music. And the label can own it forever. Sure, you'll get royalties — and so will they. Do you really want to give up the ownership of your masters for the rest of your life?

I've heard of some artists, especially the bigger-name ones, removing the perpetuity clause and instead agreeing to license their records long-term, for a period of around 20 to 25 years. That's still a really long time — but at least they get their work back at some point.

If you have the leverage, I really recommend you remove the perpetuity clause. The only time where it's acceptable in a contract is when it relates to TV, film or video game synchronizations. If a company wants to use your song in a particular scene of a film or on the credits of a TV show, they're going to want to have it forever. That's understandable. And it works for you too; you'll continue to get paid a royalty whenever that scene or those credits are played in cinemas, on TV, or when they stream online.

Here's something else to consider when it comes to the word perpetuity — and I know this has happened to other artists: what if you sign a contract that gives ownership of your record to the label, and they never put that record out? You record it, turn it in, and... it gets shelved.

This is what happened to legendary Hip Hop MC Rakim. He signed with Dr. Dre's Aftermath Records – the label hip hop fans salivate for. The album *Oh My God* had a planned release date for 2002 but it never saw the light of day because of artistic differences between Rakim and Dr.Dre.

When you sign for perpetuity, the label own your record forever, so you can't get it back and release it with another label or even on your own, unless you can negotiate to buy it back from the label – which does happen on the rare occasion. This is where your entertainment lawyer comes in: they ask for a clause to be added to the contract which protects you. A clause which says once you hand a record in, it must be released within a certain amount of time — and if it isn't, then you get your record back. That secondary clause forces the label to release the album, or, worse-case scenario — you get it back, and release it with someone else, or on your own. Either way you keep moving forwards.

I urge you to look out for the word perpetuity in any contract that's put in front of you. When you see it, talk about it with your lawyer. Negotiate with the label. Now you understand what it means, you're empowered to make an informed choice about if you grant it or not.

> *"When you record for a label, they own that material in perpetuity, meaning that they can release, choose not to release, or repackage it any way they so choose... with or without the permission of the artist." —Edgar Winter*

ARTIST PRODUCT PURCHASES

When you sign a deal in which the label owns your masters, whether it's forever or for a certain number of years, you can't press any of your CDs yourself while you are locked into that deal. On the one hand — that's great — the label are footing that cost. But, as we looked at briefly in the section on territories, there are occasions where you might want to press CDs yourself: if you're touring, or if you want to run a promo, or even if you just want to give some to family and friends.

A lot of new artists are surprised when they first learn that they have to buy back their own music from the label, and I get it. And I also know that it's just part of the game. Welcome to the music industry!

What you're looking for on your contract here is what the purchase price or buyback price is for your CDs. It's pretty common for it to be between four and five dollars. In my opinion that is a crazy buy-back price! And again, it's also the standard.

As a side note, if you were to go independent and press the CDs yourself, you'd be looking at pressing costs of anywhere from 50 cents to $1.25, maybe $1.50 — depending on how elaborate you get with the packaging and artwork. It's just worth noting.

There is something you can do here: ask for a clause in the contract where they give you 1000 CDs right off the bat so you have the option of touring and making money for all of your hard work.

RERECORDING RESTRICTIONS

"I would tell any young artist... don't sign." — Prince

When you sign a licensing or a traditional record deal, normally the label includes a clause that doesn't allow you to rerecord any of your songs for a certain length of time. This is understandable; they want to protect themselves from a situation where one of your songs is a hit and another label approaches you to do a remix. Likewise they don't want you to remix it yourself and release it independently. In both of those cases, everyone apart from the original label is making money from the record that they (most likely) financed you to make.

While there's nothing wrong with that clause being in your contract, the key is to look at how long you're restricted from rerecording. In my opinion, anything over three years is too long. In a few years time you might want to do a live version of your album, or record certain tracks again with guest vocalists. As a creator you should have that freedom.

There are a few well-documented cases where famous musicians have protested against the restrictions in their contracts with major labels. Prince changed his name to an unpronounceable symbol and appeared onstage with the word 'Slave' written on his cheek to highlight his battle to get ownership of his music catalog back from Warner Bros. (now Warner Records). He was eventually released from the label in 1996, and in 2014 he finally got his early masters back – in exchange for releasing two new albums with the label. So deals can be done – and they can also be long, drawn out, and messy.

Keep in mind that even if you sign the rights to the masters to the label for ten years, twenty years or forever — you can still make sure there's a rerecording clause in your contract that works for you. I know one band where this worked out really well: they didn't get the full masters back for their songs, but they were allowed to rerecord them after a period of time.

If you're particularly creative and innovative and you like collaborating, make sure you pay attention to your rerecording rights. Doing new versions of old songs can be fulfilling for you and exciting for your fans — plus you can keep the masters of those new versions — and therefore keep more of the money your vision and skill have earned you.

ARTISTIC CONTROL

> *"I've never been that much of a money guy. I'm more of a film guy, and most of the money I've made is in defense of trying to keep creative control of my movies."*
> — George Lucas

Back in the day, a label I was signed with offered to make a lyric video for one of my songs. It was awful. Like really, really bad. The kind of bad where I just wanted to take it down from YouTube and never have anyone see it. It was cheap, it was basic, and I didn't want it to be associated with me as an artist. At all.

And yet there it was, out in the wild, and out of my control. I knew that anyone who saw this video would make a judgment call about me as an artist — and it was a video I had no artistic control over. If it had been sent to me by the label before it was put out, I would never have signed off on it.

But it wasn't sent to me, and it didn't have to be, because I didn't know back then that you could put a clause in a record contract that stipulates the label needs to get your prior written approval before they create anything that uses your name, your brand, your image, or your logo.

If that had been included in my contract, I would have had input in the final product that was being viewed all around the world by this point. The extra-frustrating part of this story is that I actually sent the label some cool backdrops I'd made for the video, but how they used them made the whole thing look like a cheap rush job. I still shudder at the memory… and I'm so glad that I have full creative control over everything I put out now.

But it's also good to keep in mind, especially when you're a new artist just starting out, that you won't always understand other people's ideas – and that doesn't make them bad ideas. Over the course of my career, labels have brought numerous creative ideas to the table that I didn't 'get' straight away but that were one hundred percent effective – meaning the art turned out great and there were also sales so everyone was happy!

There was one time in particular when I wished I'd taken the labels advice in regard to which song to promote to active rock radio. At the time, I was riding on a high because my sales were great and I was playing some awesome tours. I thought I had the Midas touch. The president of the label warned me how risky – and expensive – going to active rock radio was in the USA. He suggested I choose to promote one of the songs we already knew was a hit, that way we'd alleviate some of the risk involved, rather than going with an untested brand-new song. Unfortunately, I didn't listen to him. The song didn't do great. I invested approx. $40,000 of my own money on a radio campaign to promote a song which I only get 20% of sales of, and I had little to no results to show for it.

Back to artistic control. Something else to keep in mind when you give away your artistic control is what you're actually giving away; it goes beyond the quality of a video, the style of a photo shoot, or the vision for an album cover — its also about whose brand is being built every time a record is released. Is it yours or the label's? For example, when you launch a new single, where will it be premiered first — your website, or theirs? Your YouTube, or theirs?

It's important that you're building *your* image, brand and reach — not the label's. Making sure you keep artistic control means you're involved in any and all of the decision making about your brand, your songs, and your career. And why shouldn't you be?

Any label worth working with will have no issue with finding the middle ground when it comes to artistic control. And any label worth working with will be happy to enter into discussions and collaborate with you, and when the trust is there, and you know they're aligned with your vision, you'll find that you appreciate their ideas and input. I've been lucky to have that experience and I'm very grateful for it. It adds an extra and welcome dimension to the creative process.

As we reach the end of Part Three, I hope the light we're casting on the world of record contracts is illuminating the usually dark and shady corners of the industry for you. And if you do choose to seek out a record deal, I hope you're feeling empowered and informed about what you're willing to trade, and what you're not so willing to trade.

Next up we're looking at how to get in touch with labels, how to get noticed, and what you need to do to make a great impression.

PART FOUR:
HOW TO SUBMIT YOUR DEMO, MAKE CONTACTS, AND SHOW YOU'RE READY TO BE SIGNED

"I liked it when I was naïve and I thought it was just about making good music." — Sia Furler

Back in Part One, I shared my list of what I believe record labels are looking for when they're considering signing a new artist. Now I want to build on that by drilling down deeper into two of the most important things you need to demonstrate when you reach out to a label to make sure you have the best chance of getting a deal.

If I were to distil it right down for you, I'd say this:

You need to show them that your music is ready — and you need to show them that YOU are ready.

You show a label your music is ready by sending the best tracks you have: finished, high quality songs, as ready to air or stream as you can get.

And you show them you're ready by sending a professional and considered email, speaking in the language they want to hear.

These two areas are our focus for this part of the book.

Before you ever reach out to a label, I recommend you get hand-on-heart honest about how ready you are. As passionate and hungry as you may be, it's essential that you take the time to give yourself the absolute best chance you can before you begin reaching out.

I know how tempting it is to prematurely contact people in the industry when you're really thirsty to get going and make connections — because I did this myself!

Back in the nineties, I was working for an IT company when I learned that one of the guys there had a sister who worked for Sony Music. I was so stoked, thinking this could be my way in and the first step on my path to becoming an international super star.

Spoiler: it was not!

I jumped in way too soon by emailing my friend's sister the tracks I had ready at the time — and they *really* weren't in a state to be shared yet.

Needless to say, she didn't take me seriously. At all. And with good reason — I didn't know what I was talking about! As well as my music being half-ready, my email wasn't written well and all I showed her was that I was naive and unprepared.

I'm so glad it doesn't have to be that way for you, and so happy I get to share with you my advice for giving you the best chance of being signed when you send that demo off.

Let's do this!

GETTING YOUR DEMO READY

Imagine you're an A&R person working at a record label. You get dozens, if not hundreds, of emails a week from artists hoping to catch your attention, hoping you'll take a chance and listen to the music they're sending over.

Are you more likely to give your time and attention to the email that says:

Hey man, check out this song. We've still got to mix it. Still going to master it or whatever, but hope you dig it, man.

Or the one that says:

Hey, we just finished this song. It's mixed and mastered. This producer wrote on it. This guest vocalist is featured on it. And I hope you check it out and hope you dig it. Let me know what you think.

I'm sure you don't need me tell you which email is most likely to motivate someone to follow a link and hit play, and which one is most likely to be ignored.

The truth is, if you send a below-par track to a record label you're just giving them a reason to reject you. And there's just so much competition for a spot on a label that you don't want to give them the slightest hint of a reason to choose someone else over you.

When someone at a record company listens to your music, they really don't want to be imagining how great it could maybe perhaps one day be. They don't want to have to fill in the blanks. They want to hear a finished product, because if they like it — they'll want to move on it. They'll want to act on it.

Your track needs to be mixed, mastered, and have no rough vocals on it

Don't send a raw demo or a rough idea you're working on with your acoustic guitar or piano (that's for your producers ears only)

Don't send something recorded into your iPhone.

Do send finished songs that have awesome production values — that means the sound quality is on par with what you hear on radio or featured on Spotify. And there's a really simple way to suss this out — and it's something I still do myself in the studio before I send a track out:

You compare your track with another track that's a hit in your genre.

When you do this, you're not deciphering if your songwriting, or the composition, or the lyrics are as good as what else is out there — because they are, right? What you're comparing is the sound quality. That means listening to the mixing and the mastering and making sure you're at the same level, and reaching the same high bar.

It takes minutes to do this. When your track is as finished as you can make it, go to Spotify or iTunes, select your genre, find out what's in the Top Ten, choose a song, and play it.

Listen to it ... and then play yours.

How does it compare? If your track sounds tinny, or hissy, or the vocals are too quiet or too loud, it's not ready.

Take action and get it ready. Iron out the glitches, the pops, the hisses. If you don't know how to do this, hire a producer or an engineer who does. One thing I love about Spotify is that it easily allows you to get the song info including the credits of who produced a song. Not all artists enter this info but a lot do so you can easily find out who produced a track and Google them to reach out and work with.

As excited as you may be about an awesome song or album you created, don't just fire it out. You owe it to yourself, your talent and your ambition to not be the person who does that.

Do it right. Strive for excellence. Send your best songs, mixed, mastered and sounding like dynamite — and blow their freaking minds!

Side note: Avoid Using Samples in Your Songs

For a lot of artists, myself included, sampling records is part of the creative process and it might even have been a rite of passage. The first track I created featured samples from old vinyl records, and my producer friends and beat-maker friends all did this back in the day. It was the norm to sample records — little snippets of vocals, drums, violins, trumpets — and mold them into our own creations. We'd put anything that sounded cool in the track, allowing pure creativity to flow with no limits.

This was, of course, until it came time to put the record out for sale. Then all of a sudden we realized if we sampled someone famous we could get into a lot of trouble if it wasn't cleared.

THE TRUTH ABOUT THE MUSIC BUSINESS

These days I know that if you want to sample a big artist you've got to have a massive budget to clear those samples, and it's a very time-consuming process. I really don't recommend it and I advise you to avoid it, and I definitely advise that you don't use samples which haven't been cleared in any of the songs you send out in your demo to a label. There are so many legal factors at play here, and if you forget to declare something as a sample, or if you haven't got it cleared yet, there's every chance you'll be facing a lawsuit. I've heard so many horror stories around this subject that I just straight up tell new artists to avoid it.

I once heard about an artist who was just about to release an album, and they were playing some of the tracks for the label. Everyone was pretty excited and it seemed like this one song in particular had real hit potential. However, as they were listening, a lawyer happened to be walking by. He popped his head around the door and said, "You can't release that — there's a sample of XXX artist in there."

The label hadn't even noticed it. And worse, the artist hadn't told them. It pushed back the release date of the album and really screwed up the relationship between the artist and their team for a while.

I find it interesting that apparently Eminem gets little to no royalties on *My Name* Is because the famous beat that drives the track is a sample from a 1975 song by Labi Siffre called I Got The... But in this instance, everyone was in the picture, permission was granted, and no copyright or plagiarism laws were broken.

When you use 100% your own music and create your own original samples you are really in the driving seat of your career because your material is yours. 100% yours. There are no conflicts, no controversy, and no legal terrains to navigate.

I know that a lot of hip hop, EDM or track-based music artists use samples and if that's you I hope you don't think I'm mashing up your vibe. As I said, I get that using samples, and even rhyming over somebody else's track is part of the creative process for a lot of artists, but you really have to tread carefully here. If you're inspired by someone else's music, make sure you really switch things up if you want to do something similar. Flow with the creative vibe to a point — but then for the final track, change it up so that it's unique, it's different and it's yours. No legal issues, no worries. You'll sleep more soundly at night, I guarantee it!

SEEKING FEEDBACK

"You can't share big dreams with small-minded people."
— Steve Harvey

If you're in this for the long haul, and you're serious about leveling up throughout your career, then getting feedback when your songs are ready to be heard is a key part of the journey of the evolving musician. I recommend you start playing your songs for other people before you reach out to a label, and — crucially — that you get particular about who you share your music with. There's a difference between the feedback you'll get from your mom or your best friend, versus the feedback you'll get from a fellow artist or industry professional.

If you're looking for reassurance and positivity, play your music for the members of your family and friendship group who you know will be supportive. It's okay to get encouragement — but realize the limitations of this kind of feedback, too. They're telling you what you want to hear, because they care about you and want you to feel good. And that's nice ... but it's only going to get you so far.

To keep moving on and moving up, we need to share our music with people who can give us constructive feedback. And I don't mean the so-called friends who have their own agenda and want to discourage you. You know who those folks are. I had a friend like that in my past, and whenever I played a song for him he'd tell me he didn't like it, or he'd be nonchalant about it, and I'd always end up wondering why I was sharing such a personal piece of myself with someone who really didn't have my best interests in mind. I would have welcomed constructive criticism from him, but he wasn't the kind of person who would, or could, deliver that.

Constructive criticism allows you to step outside of yourself a little, and be as objective as you can about what you created. It's the type of criticism that has the potential to make your songs better, and it's delivered in an honest straightforward way with no drama and no agenda — whether the agenda is to make you feel good, like your family, or bad, like a less-than-helpful or competitive friend. And you're only going to get that level of valuable feedback from people who actually know what they're talking about and understand what it is that you want to achieve with your music.

And, I have to be honest with you, sometimes feedback hurts, even when it's delivered with the best of intentions. It can be especially hard to take when you first start seeking it out. But you get more used to it with every record, and the bigger your catalog gets, the more you learn.

Find your group of people to share your music with, your trusted fellow musicians who have similar goals — especially if they're ahead of you, and call on any producers you know and any music industry experts. Make a list of people you think will give you honest, positive critiques of your songs. Tell them what the purpose of your song is, whether its a radio song, a heavy metal song, a song that you want to play live, or a song that's telling a specific story, and ask them to be honest about what works for them and what doesn't.

Another reason it's good practice to seek feedback from trusted sources before you start reaching out to labels, and before you start working with one, is because labels don't mince their words — if you're signed with them and they don't like your current track, they'll tell you, and so will radio. I always recommend you play your music for the radio promoters before the radio directors get to hear it, to get their take. They know what they're talking about so it's wise to listen.

If it seems like I'm flying ahead a little here — to the world where you're getting feedback from your label and your songs are being considered for radio — take what I'm saying in a broader sense. I just want you to prepare yourself for the world of criticism, because believe me — when you put yourself and your art out there, you'll get criticism of all varieties. So seeking out the valuable kind, and getting used to hearing it, is a really good move. Develop the thick skin now, my friend.

MAKING CONTACTS: MUSIC CONFERENCES AND EVENTS

So: Your music is ready, polished, and you're feeling pretty pumped about reaching out and sharing it with a record label. But how do you know who to reach out to? How do you make connections in such a huge multi-faceted industry, one that can seem daunting and hard to access for those on the outside looking in?

Be assured there are ways, in fact — several ways. Remember that we live in an age of connection with a host of information at our fingertips. You might even have started writing up a list of record labels or influential people you want to reach out to. The very fact that you're reading this book, and that you're this far into it, tells me you're willing to do your own research and find the people who you think could help your career.

Because that's how we begin: we get curious. We look to the artists we admire in our genre and we check out who they're signed and working with. We find those business contact details online, and, when the time is right, we reach out.

We can also widen our search by looking into industry conferences and events and, if possible, attending any that we can.

Conferences are an excellent way to make connections. There are two that I personally have found incredibly useful and formative for my career, and I always recommend both of these events to any musicians who are looking to make contacts in the industry. Events like this are around the globe — so get online and search for any that are happening near you.

The two that I'd like to draw your attention to are the ASCAP (American Society of Composers, Authors and Publishers) Expo, and the Canadian Music Week Festival. Both are among the best conferences I've ever attended for songwriters, composers, artists, and producers. They're open to everyone, whichever stage of your career you're at, and they're a great place to network and meet industry people.

It has to be said that in recent times, how we meet and the ease at which we can, and can't, travel has changed in a pretty big way. Events and conferences have had to innovate in how they reach people, by either going fully online or offering online streaming alongside their in-person events. Obviously, things can change pretty swiftly — so if you're interested in attending check the websites of both of these events for up-to-date information.

While it's a huge positive that the information and discussions from these conferences are shared so readily online, if you can make it to an in-person event I highly recommend it. Meeting people face-to-face and connecting in person is so powerful.

Other conferences I recommend you look up are South by Southwest in Austin, Texas; North by Northeast in Toronto; Reeperbahn in Germany; Music Matters in Singapore; Winter Music Conference in Florida; Midem in Cannes, France; and CD Baby's DIY Musician Conference, which is in Austin, Texas and is super cheap to get into.

Next up I'm going to share my tips for making the most of these events, and also share how you can use them as a starting point even if you can't attend in person.

Before you go to a conference

In terms of preparation, the big thing you want to do is to go to the conference website and **study the panelists.** You'll likely see there are publicists, producers and record label execs there — plus all kinds of other people who work in the industry. Think about who you really want to listen to, and who you really want the chance to speak to. Google them, look them up on LinkedIn, look at their socials, and find out all you can about them. Make notes.

CHRIS GREENWOOD

When I went to Midem in France several years ago, attendees were given a book with thousands of music professional contacts for the exact purpose of emailing them ahead of the conference to set up meetings. This is how I did multiple record deals with international record labels from all over the world.

Even without a list of contacts you can get online and do your own research. Draw up a list of who you want to connect with, and get familiar with what they look like, too. If you happen to pass them in a hallway or see them at a showcase, you want to be able to seize that opportunity to have a quick conversation.

Quick being the word, here — which is why you also need to **prepare a 60-second elevator pitch**. In those 60 seconds, you introduce yourself, sell yourself, and hopefully set up a meeting or at least share contact details. If you've already attended the person's talk, you can say how much you enjoyed it, or if it's still to come, then say you're looking forward to it. Here's a example of an elevator pitch you can tailor to your needs:

Hey, my name's _____, I've sold _____records / got _____streams / just lined up a tour with _____/ about to shoot this crazy music video for my latest single. I loved hearing your take on _____, it was so enlightening. I would love to connect with you / send you my music / or just tell my story. Can I buy you lunch / a drink / send you some of my material?

Practice your pitch as much as you can before you head to the event, making it sound as natural as possible. Be friendly, direct, and remember to smile! Also think about what you can give to them as opposed to trying to take. In short: be human.

The other thing that most conferences offer, usually for an extra fee — but they are so worth it — are **one-on-one sessions** with someone in the music industry. In essence, you get to have a private meeting with someone who knows their stuff and can accelerate your career. Years ago, I booked a one-on-one with a music supervisor, and though I paid an extra couple of hundred bucks for that meeting, I ended up getting a sync placement that was worth thousands of dollars. I really encourage you to check out what the event offers in terms of one-on-one meetings and invest the extra money to sit down with someone. They give you new insights, open doors and can mark the beginning of ongoing and profitable relationships.

At the conference

When you're in an audience listening to a panel, **take notes and soak up all you can**. You're probably going to get inspired and excited just by being around all of these influential and prominent people, but keep your cool! You want to keep your feet on the ground and be rooted in the present moment so you can **recognize any opportunities that come up**, especially if it's an opportunity to speak to one of the people you're interested in. Whether you see them in the hallway or grab a chance to speak to them after their talk, be cool, be courteous — and **deliver your elevator pitch**.

If your conversation doesn't close with them agreeing to meeting, at the very least you want to get their business card so you can follow up (but don't offer yours unless they ask for it). That way, when you send a follow up email in a few days, you have an 'in', and you can refer to the fact you met them in person and had a conversation.

Honestly, these events are such awesome investments for your career. If you can attend one, make the most of it. Get the one-on-one, listen, learn, and seize any opportunities that come your way. Oh, and have fun. This is your industry, and these are your people!

After the conference

Follow up! Email anyone that you spoke to, had a meeting with, connected with. Capitalize on any connections you made. In your email you can say something like:

Hey, this is _____, we chatted on Saturday right after your panel on _____, which was so refreshing and motivating. I just wanted to reach out and share that music video with you...

There's more coming on how to write a great email, and how to follow up, in the next couple of pages.

If you can't make it in-person

If, for whatever reason, getting to one of these events or conferences isn't possible for you right now, the websites themselves are still a good source of information. Go to the list of speakers and panelists, and see who looks interesting and who you sense would be good to connect with. Use a search engine to find their business contact details, and send an email over. Again, I have lots to share on how best to reach out by email coming right up.

Also, if you're not already on LinkedIn, I really recommend you create an account and start building a profile — it's basically Facebook for business networking. As well as being a great way to connect with people, it's also a useful way to look up contacts. I've used this so many times to connect with people I'm interested in working with.

I hope it goes without saying that you're not just going to start randomly hitting people up just because you can! Any communication you initiate needs to have a purpose, and you need to be professional and give yourself the best chance of getting a reply.

Let's look at how we can do that next.

HOW TO EMAIL A RECORD LABEL — AND GET A RESPONSE

"Be so good they can't ignore you." — Steve Martin

If you recall, back at the start of this section, I noted that the way to demonstrate to a record label that you're ready to be signed is by sending music that's polished and ready to stream, and also by *sending a professional and considered email, speaking in the language they want to hear.*

That's what we're going to look at in this chapter. I just want to point out that the principles I'll share here are not exclusive to emailing record labels only. You can use them to guide you when you contact anyone in the industry that you're hoping to meet or work with.

If you think about it, we want three things to happen when we send an email out in any professional capacity.

The first is that we want the recipient to actually open our email. Okay, that might sound obvious! But seriously — it's possible that your contact gets hundreds of emails a day. And a lot of them are from wannabe artists who aren't actually serious about their careers – but you are! When they're scrolling through their unread messages, you want yours to actually pass the first hurdle by not being ignored or deleted.

The second thing that we want is for our recipient to read the email and think, *Yes — this person gets it.* This is what I mean when I say we need to 'speak the language they want to hear.' You want them to know that you're intelligent, that you have an awareness of how the music business works, and that you're dedicated to your career — whichever stage you're at.

Finally we want them to respond. All of the advice in this chapter is going to set you up for the best chance of getting a response to any email you send out, whether it's to a label, a producer, a manager, a radio station, a journalist, or anyone else you want to work with or have on your team.

Before you write your email

Before you start composing the body of your email, make sure you get clear on what your intention is for getting in touch with whoever you're reaching out to. Ask yourself, *What's the purpose of this email?*

Do you want to secure a meeting, get them to come and see you play live, play your song on the radio, or simply start a dialogue?

Whatever your specific reason for reaching out is, it's useful to have in mind that the general, over-arching purpose of this email is to get the attention of the recipient, and to show that you have something to share that you hope will be of interest or value to them.

With that in mind, let's take a deeper dive into how to put together an email that's going to have the best chance of leading to a response from a record company.

First: Nail the subject line

The whole purpose of a subject line is to get the person you're emailing to open the email. You either want your subject line to impress them or intrigue them. Or both!

The quickest way to impress is by referring to any relevant accolades or achievements you have in the music industry — however big or small. If it's a booking agent you're contacting, the subject line should be about selling tickets. If it's a label, maybe it's how many streams you have.

So your subject line might be something like:

We just did a sell-out show — here's our new single featuring [BIG artist]

5000 streams and counting...

Just featured on [Insert TV Show].

Don't worry if you're in the early stages of your career and you don't have any accolades or achievements to share just yet. This is where you get to be intriguing, or mysterious, or a little quirky, in your subject line.

Examples of an intriguing subject line might look like this:

Did we just make the weirdest music video ever?

Invitation: High school geek now making beats — dancing awkwardly on a stage near you this Friday!

Have fun and be playful, remembering that it's really likely the person reading your email has another 50 waiting to be opened, deleted or ignored — this is you doing what you can to stay out of the trash!

Something else that can intrigue or inspire someone to open your email is if you take a personal angle, and this works especially well if the two of you have some kind of connection already. Here's an example of from my own career. A while ago, I was reaching out to someone in the industry who I realized went to the same high school as me.

My subject line for that email was:

Four-time JUNO Award nominee, Manafest - AKA Chris Greenwood from Pine Ridge

By citing a common connection, I hoped to make this guy curious. Even if he didn't remember me, I wanted him to pause and recognize his hometown, and be intrigued enough to open the email.

The connection you have with your recipient doesn't need to be as solid as my example. You might be emailing someone whose career you've followed, or someone you saw speaking at a conference. In that case, you could personalize your subject line with something like:

So inspired by your talk at ASCAP Experience

However you choose to compose the subject line, keep this in mind: You have one goal — and it's to make your recipient think: Okay, tell me more.

One last tip is to never have more than seven words in your subject line. Obviously, some of my examples have more than seven... so be willing to break that rule!

Next: How to write the body of your email

The body of your email needs to be short and to the point. No rambling sentences, no long and dense paragraphs. You want short sentences, plenty of white space, and you need to ensure you only include what's relevant.

I'm going to share some examples in a moment that you can adapt for your own use, but in essence a succinct and professional email to get a record label interested in you will follow a structure that goes like this:

- Begin by addressing the person by name who you're writing to (and please, please get their name right! Check and double-check the spelling)

- Introduce yourself

- Mention a relevant achievement, or anything that makes you stand out (this might be your unique story - something we looked at back in Part One of the book)

- Say that you have some songs that you think would fit into the label's output and ethos — and you'd love to hear what they think

- Add a link to those songs

- Add anything else that's relevant, like if you've got a show coming up, you can say you'd be happy to put them on the guest list. Or if you've been featured on TV or radio or a podcast, you can add the link and invite them to check it out

- Sign off with your name and direct contact number

- Add a signature at the end of the email (more on that coming up)

I'll now share with you two ways I'd write this kind of email: one that I'd write now, at this point in my career, and another that I might have written earlier in my career, back when I first started seriously looking for a label to work with.

The email I'd write now

SUBJECT LINE A: Manafest, Four-time JUNO Award Nominee

SUBJECT LINE B: Manafest – 900,000 monthly listeners

Hey David

This is Chris Greenwood A.K.A Manafest.

I'm a rock artist from Toronto, Canada, with over 900,000 monthly listeners on Spotify.

We just released a new song that got over 100,000 streams in one week.

Would love to chat about partnering together on some new music and taking it to the next level.

Here's a link to my music on Spotify:

[Spotify link]

And if you want to download the MP3, here's the Dropbox link:

[Dropbox link]

Also we're playing at [venue] Friday 6th May — would be awesome if you wanted to come down. Let me know and I'll add you to the guest list!

Look forward to hearing from you,

Chris

[Direct phone number]

The email I'd have written when I was first looking to get signed

SUBJECT LINE: Inspired by your talk at ASCAP Experience

Hey David

This is Chris Greenwood A.K.A Manafest.

I'm a rock artist from Toronto, Canada, and I saw your interview at ASCAP Experience.

It was so awesome and inspiring, I could sense the exhilaration in the whole audience.

I have a new single coming out in July, and we just made a really cool but pretty crazy video to go with it!

I'd love you to check it out, and maybe I can take you out for lunch next week sometime?

I'll be in town from Monday.

If you have time, let me know. You can get me on: [Direct phone number].

Here's a link to the music video:

[YouTube link]

Here's my music on Spotify:

[Spotify link]

And if you want to download the MP3, here's the Dropbox link:

[Dropbox link]

Look forward to hearing from you,

Chris

What do you think of these two examples? What I really wanted you to get from the second email is that you don't need to have awards or hundred of thousands of streams to sound impressive and professional. The second email shows that you know what you're talking about, that you've been building the foundations of your career, and that you believe you have something of value to share with your recipient.

Two extra ways to stand out and avoid the trash can

1. Never attach a file

Did you notice how I shared the music in the emails above? With links. The links will either take the recipient to a streaming service like Spotify, or to a video on YouTube, or to Dropbox where they can opt to download the track if they want. This is the safest, easiest, and most welcome way of sharing your music by email.

Never attach a file. Whether it's MP3 or a WAV or an AIFF — they're big, they take up too much space and they slow email applications right down. Honestly attaching a music file is the best way to get your email deleted or hidden away forever in a spam folder. Especially an unsolicited email.

Sending a Dropbox link is easy and safe, and it's the industry norm. If you don't have a Dropbox account already, I highly recommend it. I use the app on my phone as well, so if I'm away from the studio and my music supervisor needs an instrumental sent over, or someone on my team needs a press photo, I have access to all the files I need and I can share them quickly and with ease.

Unless you're specifically asked to send a file, don't do it!

2. Add a pro signature at the end of your email

Your email signature is the information that appears at the end of every email you send. It's like a calling card. I always include my name, a tagline, and some nugget of up-to-date information about what I'm doing. Then I have links to all my socials and my website, and my contact details.

So that might look like this:

Chris Greenwood A.K.A Manafest
Four-time Juno Award nominee, author, and over 1000 shows rocked on four continents.
New album coming Fall 2022
[Links to website, socials, YouTube]
[Cell phone number]

I recommend including your cell because it makes getting in touch with you as easy as possible. Notice that in the two example emails I just shared, my cell number is actually included in the body of the email, either just after my name (the first one) or within the invitation to have lunch (the second). I did this because I think it makes it clear you're happy to be contacted directly, which not all people are — so this is another way to stand out and show you're serious.

Okay, let's recap. You know your email is ready because:

- You have a clear reason for reaching out.
- You've come up with a killer subject line.
- You've composed a succinct, well-written, personal yet professional email.
- You've included the relevant links to your music.
- Your signature showcases you as the pro that you are.
- There is no attachment.

WAIT! Before you hit send...

If you've followed the steps shared here, then it's likely you've already done more prep than half of the emails your recipient is going to open today.

That puts you in a really great position.

So please, don't throw that away by hitting send on a whim before you've checked the email over. Proofread it for any spelling mistakes, grammar issues, or missing words. If you're not too confident with that kind of thing, ask a friend to take a look. Otherwise, you can always pause and come back to it with fresh eyes the next day. I have one buddy who actually told me to stop sending emails late at night! When I email late at night there are bound to be spelling errors and grammar issues. When I wait until the next morning, I see them clearly and correct them. After all of your hard work – don't let a few spelling errors make you look any less professional than you are.

THE FORTUNES ARE IN THE FOLLOW UP

"One immediate action is better than one thousand good intentions."— Stephen Furtick

Whenever you send an email in a professional capacity and it doesn't get a reply, whether it's to someone you met at a conference or a new contact you're initiating yourself, make sure you follow up with another email. And then another. And maybe another.

Persistence is the key here. Let go of any apprehensions you have that following up is annoying or that you'd be bothering someone. As long as you're polite and considerate, it's totally fine to follow up on emails that haven't had a response yet. People are busy, and sometimes they need a little nudge.

My advice is to leave a week between follow ups. After your initial email, wait a week and then send something like:

Hey, I just wanted to follow up to see if you had a chance to listen to that song yet / check out the music video / watch me performing live?

If another week passes and you still haven't heard back from them, then try this:

Hey, I just wanted to follow up on the email below...

And then copy and paste your email from the previous week, or the first week, whichever you prefer. I've done this myself for several weeks in a row, just following up and following up and following up.

If a music career is something you want, you have to pursue these leads and connections. My advice is to always be persistent and go after what you want. One trick I do is to put their first name in the subject line, or even a "Yo".

WHAT TO DO IF YOU GET A 'NO'

First, understand that 'No' is a part of the journey. I've heard the word 'No' so many times, and when you first start looking for a label to work with you're pretty likely to face your own set of rejections. Learn that every time you hear a 'No', you're just one step closer to a 'Yes'.

Usually, when it comes from a label, a 'No' is phrased as a 'not right now', or 'our roster is full'. My advice is to never let that discourage you from staying in touch and building a relationship with that person. So many artists hear 'No' and then never touch base with that person again. I think this is the biggest mistake you could possibly make.

Whether it's a label you're in touch with or someone else in the industry, see the reaching out process like you're courting them. That's how I see it, and it's the approach I take when I'm hoping to get a chance to work with a particular person.

When you really want to work with someone, email them about once a month just with an update on what you're doing and creating and putting out there. Don't keep sending the same song or the same information over and over, keep it fresh and show that you're active.

You could say something like:

Hey, I was just on this show last week. It went really, really well. Here's a link to it. I know you're busy but would love your thoughts.

Or,

Hey, we just got back from this tour with _____ and it was such a ride. Just wanted to check in. We'd still love to meet with you.

The aim is to just keep building a rapport. I've done that with so many people. And then finally — finally — I got a response and it opened up another door.

Understand that what you're asking from someone is their time, and that's the most valuable asset they own. When you do get a piece of someone's time, make sure you respect it and make sure you're prepared. If you get a meeting set up, know what you want from it.

Eventually, as you keep pushing forward and not quitting, you're going to get a breakthrough and the doors are going to open. If you're persistent and you keep at this, you keep creating music, you keep marketing it, you keep networking and getting out and meeting people, you're going to be successful in this industry.

Keep climbing — because you're climbing the ladder towards your dreams.

PART FIVE:
PERSISTENCE PAYS

"If you can't fly then run, if you can't run then walk, if you can't walk then crawl, but whatever you do you have to keep moving forward." — Martin Luther King Jr.

I called my first book Fighter because cultivating and calling on a fighting spirit is what's got me to where I am today. From losing my father to suicide when I was five, to losing my dream of being a pro skateboarder in my late teens, to reinventing myself as a musician and the many and multiple knock backs that come with this life choice — I know what it is to fall, and I know how important it is to keep getting back up.

I'm certain that by now you understand that if you want to make it in this industry, you need to dig deep and find that willingness to keep going, keep moving forward, and keep fighting for your dream.

You will get rejected, you will make mistakes, and sometimes you'll give it all you've got and still the dice just won't roll in your favor. And you won't be alone: some of the biggest stars on the planet were once on the brink of obscurity — and they kept going, kept moving forward, and went on to live the life of their dreams.

Among them:

- Eminem — whose debut album only sold 1000 copies

- Elvis Presley — who was told he should go back to driving trucks

- Jay Z — who sold CDs out of his car when he couldn't get signed by a label

- Kanye West — who, when he worked as a producer at Roc-A-Fella records, had to persuade them to sign him as an artist … And they only agreed because they didn't want to lose him as a producer

- Pharrell — whose first album wasn't a hit — and it took him eight years to release the next one

- Ed Sheehan — who was rejected by several labels because of his looks

There are hundreds more stories like this of artists who were rejected or faced struggle early in their careers and are now household names: The Beatles, Madonna, U2, Beyoncé, Lady Gaga, Dave Grohl... every one of these global stars or bands suffered knock backs and refused to give up.

As hard as this industry can be to crack, the fact you are here reading this book shows you're prepared to learn and tool yourself up. If you couple that preparedness with persistence and grit, plus the willingness to fight for the future you came here to live — you WILL make it.

You've already made a huge investment in yourself just by being here, arming yourself with the knowledge you need to forge your career. If you stay focused on your vision and if you're always willing to keep moving, keep learning and keep growing — your day will come, and success will come.

It's all there for the taking, my friend. It really is.

MY STORY

I want to close the book by bringing us back around to the subject of labels and record deals, by sharing with you the story of how I got signed, and a couple of insights about what went wrong, what went right, and where I am now. Some of this I've mentioned earlier in the book, but here's the full story in one place.

CHRIS GREENWOOD

Back when I first started looking to work with a label it was the early nineties, and I'm the first to admit I was naive, wide-eyed, and I just really wanted people to believe in me. I'd discovered a passion for music after suffering a skateboarding injury, and painting my pain with lyrics got me through losing that dream while helping to spin me a new one: to be a musician, and to share my music with the world. That dream became my driving force, and having the backing of a label was all part of that early vision.

So in 2005 when I inked my first deal, with a label based out of Seattle (with distribution through EMI) I had hope in my heart that this was it: my time had come and my dream was coming to fruition. By this point, I'd been making music, playing shows, and had released an EP and a full-length album all under my own steam.

I'll remind you here although this was the first deal I signed, it wasn't the first I was offered: I'd already walked away from a few others which were dodgy to say the least. Luckily I'd got some friends in the industry as well as a lawyer to look those first deals over, and the advice I received was very much, "Walk away". In all honesty, without that advice, I might have signed those early deals just because the people pushing the paper toward me seemed to believe in me. I'm so glad I didn't.

So, when the Seattle label came along and made me an offer for a licensing deal for three albums, I simultaneously wanted to be careful while also knowing in my gut I was beyond ready to be signed and get my career going. After about a year of negotiations, my lawyer looked the contract and said, "This is about the best you're going to get."

The thing was, he was right: I didn't have any leverage to negotiate further. I'd only really toured in Canada, and played a few shows in the US. I'd released one independent EP and one album, didn't have any radio, didn't have a huge number of sales, or a history of tickets sold. The label liked me, liked my music, saw my potential — but I wasn't in a position of power at all.

So, although there was no advance, and it wasn't a full deal, I signed. Despite it not being the deal of my dreams, it was still a pivotal moment, and one of celebration. I remember dancing around our condo with my wife, both of us full of wanderlust about how our lives were going to change.

And they did change — but the dream I was chasing wasn't ready to show up just yet. In my excitement to get things moving, I quit my job with its $70,000 salary, and went on tour, and... pretty much went broke pretty quickly. It wasn't until I learned how to make money by playing shows and selling merchandise afterward that I had an income. It was a real learning curve: I was sleeping on the side of the road, sleeping on hotel room floors, just trying to figure out this music industry and what works. Without a salary I had to rely strictly on music to pay the bills. Talk about a wakeup call!

Within a few months I was $30,000 in debt. It took many years to pay that back, but help came when — *at last* — I had my big break. My second record with the label blew up in Japan, selling over 10,000 albums a week, and breathing new life into my career.

After I'd put out that second record on my contract, the success I was having in Japan put me in the powerful position of being able to meet with EMI Japan directly and ask if they'd be interested in doing a deal with me. I proposed a one-album deal, and I had so much more to bargain with now: I'd released three albums with the label, had great sales, a growing fanbase, good social media numbers, and multiple tours under my belt.

EMI Japan were quick to agree with my offer, which admittedly didn't go down too well with the label in the USA who I was essentially cutting out. The label in the USA wanted to capitalize on my success in Japan by cutting a deal that only included Japan — not the US.

It's easy to see why that's what they wanted: I was barely making any sales in the US. And why? Because they weren't pushing or supporting me there. They wanted in on the success I was making happen in Japan — and I didn't feel they deserved a slice of that pie. The US was the only territory that I wanted my deal with the label in the USA to cover, and I stuck to my guns.

They were reluctant but eventually agreed when they heard the songs off the record they'd be signing me for, predicting that one song in particular, Avalanche, would be a hit. There was a caveat: a lyric change to make it appropriate for radio ("You scared the hell out of me" became "You scared the junk out me") which I gladly agreed with — and they were right: Avalanche was my first radio hit in the USA, selling 100,000 singles and while the album hit well over 50,000 copies.

The label sure changed their tune quickly when I became a hit in the USA. It wasn't too long before our tour went through Seattle and my wife and I were having dinner and drinks with the president. Before I was a success it was Thai food at the whole-in-the-wall joint downtown ... which actually was epic and the best Thai food ever! Anyways.

In the same way I did a deal direct with EMI Japan, I also went directly to a label in India, Germany, the UK, and Canada, each time with no middle man.

However, there was one aspect of the contract I forgot to negotiate — and you might have seen this coming from what I shared in Part Three of the book — and it was the term. Despite all the leveraging power I now had, I neglected to consider how long the label would own my record for.

I signed too hastily, feeling the pressure because the release date was set in Japan and we needed a US partner. We were actually in talks with multiple major labels including EMI but they were taking too long. So in a rush I resigned with the label I had previously worked with and forgot to look at the term of the deal. Although it was just a one-record deal, they had rights to that record for seven long years. And, it just happened to be the record that accelerated my career and took my success to a whole new level.

But... you live and learn. Or, I learned "the hard way", so you don't have to.

I eventually went independent in 2015, and I've never looked back. I own 100% of my music, have full artistic control, and have assembled the best team around me who support and work with me on a daily basis so I can keep doing what I love and sharing it with the world.

I can hand-on-heart say that I am living my dreams. I love making music, I love playing live, I love connecting with fans, and I get to do at least one and sometimes all of those things every day.

Having said all of that, I have to be real and honest with you. The only reason I'm still here doing music full-time is because I pushed through. It's not because I'm the most talented. I'm here because I persisted, and I wanted it badly enough to keep going. There were way more talented rappers and singers out there, artists I saw almost make it but then stagger, stumble, and fall — and they didn't get back up. Whether they didn't want it badly enough, or didn't want to grow and learn and adapt, I'm not sure. It's not for me to judge.

I just want YOU to know that yes — this industry can seem like the hardest to get into, but people break through all the time, in all manner of ways.

I'd like to end the book with the same question I started with, and invite you to take a moment to see if your perception of labels and contracts has changed at all.

Here it is:

Why do you want a record deal?

And, expanding on that:

What can a label do for you that you can't do on your own?

I hope you've gained some new insights as you've journeyed with me through these pages, and if a record deal is still part of your dream, you now have the information and awareness to ensure you look for and sign a deal that works for you.

Finally, please always hold fast to your dream and your vision of being a successful music artist — whatever that looks like for you, and whichever route you decide to take.

Good luck, my friend. I look forward to hearing or streaming you soon!

For more advice and coaching 1-on-1 visit Smartmusicbusiness.com/coaching to book a call.

Also make sure to watch the free training: How I hit over 900,000 Monthly Listeners on Spotify Without a Record Deal and No Touring at: Smartmusicbusiness.com/spotifywebinar

ADDITIONAL BOOKS BY CHRIS GREENWOOD

Music Business & Marketing Accelerator: *Grow Your Fanbase Using Instagram & Launch Your Career in The New Music Industry*

From Red to Black: *A Short Journey from Debt to Liberty*

How to Write and Release Your First Song: *Songwriting Secrets from an Award-Winning Artist*

Music Marketing Promotions Guide: *Over 21 Tested and Proven Hollywood Marketing Strategies to Promote Every Song You Release*

Spotify Profits: *How I Got 100,000 Followers and 12 Million Streams Marketing My Music on Spotify*

Teach What You Know: *A 12 Step Guide to Creating Your First Online Course & Earning Passive Income*

YouTube Playbook for Artists & Musicians: *Start Getting More Views, Comments, Royalties and Subscribers on Your YouTube Channel*

COURSES AND RESOURCES BY CHRIS GREENWOOD

Active Campaign Five-Day Free Trial & 10x Your Fanbase Five-Day Challenge: https://www.10xyourfanbase.com/100kfans

Fanbase University: https://fanbaseuniversity.com/

Smart Music Business: https://smartmusicbusiness.com/

Smart Music Business Funnel Training: https://smartmusicbusiness.com/freefunnel

www.ingramcontent.com/pod-product-compliance
Lightning Source LLC
Chambersburg PA
CBHW052308300426
44110CB00035B/2199